To: Chris

Keep on Winning.

Tim

1/30/09

HOPE

Winning
With
Millennials

Attracting, Retaining, and Empowering
the Next Generation of
Design Firm Professionals

BY: J. TIM GRIFFIN, PE, LEED AP

Winning With Millennials: Attracting, Retaining, and Empowering the Next Generation of Design Firm Professionals

Design Leadership Press | A Division of
PSMJ│Resources, Inc.®
P.O. Box 95190
Nonantum, MA 02495
Phone: 617-965-0055
Fax: 617-965-5152
Email: customerservice@psmj.com
www.psmj.com

ISBN 1-55538-247-9

Manufactured in the United States of America.

ACKNOWLEDGEMENTS

I want to first dedicate this book to my loving wife, who sacrificed time with me while I researched and wrote it, who provides me with deep insight into people, and who always encourages me to pursue my dreams.

To my mother, who first gave me a love for reading.

To my four children — Nathan, Luba, Sarah, and Stephen — who themselves are Millennials.

To Barney, Vance, and Greg, my three Gen X leaders, who make me look much better in business than I am.

And to Aaron, Brian, Chris, Pat, Kyle, Mike, Jonathan, Rob, and Cheryl, the Millennials who drive our team's success, make work a joy, and who unknowingly contributed many quotes and material to this effort.

Thanks for believing in me!

I also want to thank all of the consultants whose expertise provided valuable insight into this subject, including Sandy Blaha, Mike D'Alessandro, Dave Burstein, and many others.

J. Tim Griffin, PE, MBA, LEED AP

Bio

J. Tim Griffin is a partner and division manager with RMF Engineering, Inc., a national engineering consulting firm operating across the United States. He is a registered professional engineer and certified energy manager with a bachelor of science in mechanical engineering from North Carolina State University and a master's degree in business administration from Colorado State University.

In his role at RMF Engineering, he served one term on the board of directors, developed leadership training programs, led geographical and practice area business development expansions, and helped plan and manage the firm's growth into international markets.

Griffin has written numerous articles on management for PSMJ Resources Inc., the industry leader in professional design firm intelligence, and trained hundreds of design firm principals across North America in best business practices.

He makes his home in Raleigh, North Carolina, with his wife Beth, and four children; all of which are Millennials.

TABLE OF CONTENTS

INTRODUCTION

"They're lazy," bemoans the head of a Pacific Northwest design firm, receiving nods of agreement from a roomful of similar leaders representing firms across North America. "They don't want to pay their dues," says another. "When its quitting time, they are out the door wanting to play. How am I supposed to run a business with people who have no concern for building a career?"

"I ask them to take on an out-of-town assignment for five weeks and they look at me like I'm crazy!" complains a design firm manager based in Ontario in his thick Canadian accent. "Don't they realize it's their #@!%& job? I had to do this all the time when I was their age!"

The "they" these design firm principals are referring to is the new generation of young professionals graduating from institutions of higher education with freshly minted architectural and engineering degrees. Over the past couple of years, I have traveled across North America leading business training sessions to hundreds of design firm professionals. From CEOs to CFOs, division managers to project managers, nothing quite puts a fire in their eyes as a discussion of the latest generation entering today's workforce.

A few years ago, some design firms refused to hire them, preferring to require some level of previous work (and life) experience. However, in my recent travels, I no longer hear this refrain. The demands of the marketplace, coupled with a rapidly growing inability to hire experienced professionals and the need to replace retiring boomers, have made hiring new graduates a necessity even in firms that are only trying to maintain current staffing levels.

So who are these so-called "Millennials"? What makes them tick? Are they really as bad as what we hear? Is there any hope for our design industry moving forward?

Eleven years ago, the firm in which I am a principal and part owner gave me the opportunity to build a team from scratch to serve a new market opportunity, a challenge I had been looking for. Knowing the biggest key to future success was directly dependent on the quality of the team's members, I decided to pursue the best young college interns and new grads, as well as the best seasoned professionals I could find. However, as the team began to grow, I quickly found more success with the younger team members.

In retrospect, there were two problems I encountered with more experienced professionals. First, even 10 years ago, firms worked very hard to hold onto their best talent. As a result, the more experienced candidates who were looking for work often did not have the qualities that would drive the success of our venture. Second, typically, more experienced team members are set in their ways and not open to change. In contrast, younger architects and engineers are more open to trying different approaches (they actually thrive on it) and are certainly more open to working on their weak points. In addition, I found within this group some of the most talented, motivated, and energetic young professionals you can imagine. For me, they make coming to work every day a joy.

I remember having a conversation years ago, as I was just beginning to build the team, with a partner from another division in our firm about the best methods to grow your team. He was convinced hiring young professionals was the wrong approach and I was making a mistake. To him, hiring more experienced professionals was a better approach. I seriously considered his argument, but something in my gut said it was wrong so I stuck to my guns. I'm sure glad I did!

Today, the team has grown from serving one new market to three, is leading the company's expansion into international markets, has had zero turnover over the past five years, has become the preferred service provider for most of our clients, has created a relatively low stress, fun work environment (it's definitely not a sweatshop), and consistently produces financial returns more than twice the industry average. Most importantly, at least to my wife and I, my stress level is as low as it has ever been! I'm having a great time and even had time to research and write this book. Still, today, my team has the lowest average age of any division in the company. Millennials, who we will learn started graduating from college at the end of the last century, are dominating the team.

As I have listened to design firm leaders across the country complain about today's generation, I have also met a handful of company leaders who are recognizing their value and harnessing their energy. As a result, their firms are growing faster than the industry as a whole, while also experiencing stellar financial returns on their investment. Many of these firms are highlighted in Chapter 9.

The purpose of this book is NOT to lay out a plan to change millennials into a Boomer or Gen Xer. I doubt that is even an achievable goal. Also, this is not meant to be an indictment of any kind regarding the parents of millennials and their parenting methods. Each generation faces new challenges to parenting based on the conditions of the world at that time. It's difficult for one generation, who understands how they learned work ethic, morals, beliefs, and skills, etc., to transfer how another generation could learn these same things in a different environment. For instance, people who lived through the Great Depression learned much from their experience and it shaped a lot of their beliefs. In talking to them, I sometimes get a sense of disbelief that anyone who did not grow up in those difficult times lacked certain qualities needed to lead. Yet, somehow, our country has continued to survive and thrive.

Instead, the purpose of this book is to develop a clear picture of how the generation now entering the workforce thinks, acts, and lives, as well as explore some of the environmental issues that shaped their thinking. Most importantly, I'm going to provide you with practical strategies to attract the best and brightest millennials to your design firms, create a culture that will be desirable to them over the short- and long-term, and propose ways to keep them motivated, productive, and fully engaged.

As previously mentioned, I am a design firm principal, born just as the Boomer Generation was ending and Generation X began. As such, I can relate somewhat to both. This book is written specifically to members of these two generations, and the ones before, who want to understand how the latest arrivals to our firms think, work, and act.

Why is this important to you? Because the firm's that successfully embrace millennials will have a growing competitive advantage over the firms that fail in this arena. Failing firms will eventually run out of talent and go out of business. I'm confident, however, if you strategically embrace this generation you will find the experience both rewarding and enjoyable, as I have.

CHAPTER 1

The Millennials

"I'm going to retire by the time I'm 35."
— Quote from a recently graduated 22-year-old
civil engineer on his first day at work.

Here's a test. What event is a defining moment in your formative years? The answer gives a clue to the generation in which you are a member:

- V-E Day
- JFK's Assassination
- The Space Shuttle Challenger Explosion
- 9/11

If you answered V-E Day, then you are most likely a member of the Veterans generation, whose members were born before 1946. If you answered JFK's assassination, you probably were born somewhere in the Baby Boomer generation, the often-studied group born between 1946 and 1963, which because of its size has had a tremendous impact on whatever segment of society they were entering.

As of late, one of our national concerns is the potential negative impact of retiring Boomers on our nation's economy, as well as our Social Security and Medicare systems. If your vivid memory is of the Challenger explosion, you're most likely a member of Generation X, which began in 1964 and continued to the end of the 1970s.

For Millennials, it's only the last one. Most were way too young, or not even born, when the Space Shuttle Challenger exploded shortly into its flight. In fact, the 2008 election marked the first time they remember when the president of the United States did not have the last name of either Bush or Clinton. When making reference to "…when E.F. Hutton speaks, everyone listens," they have no idea what you are talking about.

Their predecessors, Generation X, were the original latchkey kids, who grew up in a culture where there was reduced parental involvement as a result of higher divorce rates and the high rates of dual-income parents. Both forces led to children who often had to fend for themselves. As a result, this generation is often very independent and entrepreneurial.

There is little consensus on when Generation X ended and the next began. Most experts peg births beginning as early as 1978 and as late as 1982, through those born somewhere between 1995 and the year 2000. First they were called Generation Y because they followed Generation X. Later, other names were added, such as Generation Next and Echo Boomers, because they are the children of the Boomers. Since the Boomer generation is huge, their children's generation is also much larger than Generation X which separates the two. However, the Boomers sought lower birth rates than their Veteran generation parents. As such, although still relatively large, this latest generation is slightly smaller than that of their parents.

Their size has certainly been large enough to make its presence known. For instance, during the late 1970s and into the 1980s, little new construction occurred on our nation's campuses. Generation X was so small there existed plenty of residence halls, classroom, recreational, and support facilities to meet their needs. In fact most of these facilities had been completed to accommodate the boomer generation. When the Boomers' children began approaching college age in the late nineties, a campus construction boom began that has yet to subside. Members of Generation X often lament feeling squeezed between two more populous generations.

In 1980, Baby Boomers first dominated the workforce. Since that time, there have consistently been more Boomers in our nation's workforce than members of any other generation. With Boomers now retiring, and Millennials graduating from college in large numbers, by the year 2010, Millennials will take over the role as the most dominant part of our nation's workforce, skipping Generation X entirely. No wonder Gen Xers feel squeezed.

The relatively small size of Generation X helped lead to the lack of available talent today, specifically in that mid-range experience area. The bad news is the latest generation's size is not adequate to replace aging boomers who are just now starting to reach retirement age, nor is there a strong desire among them to join our industry.

Interestingly enough, the latest generation is the first to ever come up with its own name. Previous generations derived their names from sociological circles. This time, however, the late Peter Jennings on his ABC newscast asked people born after 1980 to give input via an online survey as to what they would like to be called. The response was very strong and overwhelmingly favored 'Millennials,' a name that ties them with the dawning of a new century. Even the process says something about them. They are independent, outspoken, and want their voice to be heard. It shouldn't be surprising they preferred not to have a name that would connect them to a previous generation.

ENVIRONMENTAL INFLUENCES

Each generation is shaped by the environment in which they are reared. Defining moments in their culture, parents' attitudes toward child rearing, even the relative affluence of society all impact their attitudes, dreams, and aspirations. Here are some of the forces that influenced the development of Millennials:

Each generation presents unique challenges to the generation before. In March 2000, Sandy Blaha, a PSMJ consultant, published this article on tips for managing and retaining Generation X. This shows not only some of the characteristics of the generation before Millennials, but also some of the challenges design firm leaders were then having in figuring out how to manage them.

"Retaining Generation Xers"

***PSMJ*, March 2000**

"Gen Xers" — the up-and-coming workforce of individuals born between 1965 and 1977 — are the smallest pool of entry workers in six decades. But this group of 21- to 33-year-olds will shape and drive the future in many businesses.

Seventy-four percent of Gen Xers agree with the statement "Hard work is the key to getting ahead." And, more than any other generation, they agree with the statement "The only really meaningful measure of success is money," according to an article by Dan Zevin in the October 1997 issue of *U.S. News and World Report*.

Developing and implementing a strategy to retain Generation X (and all your employees) is a long-term process. To be a great employer, you must create a consistent culture in which managers communicate the firm's vision and value to all employees.

Gen Xers need this information so they can see how they fit into the picture. Gen Xers grew up in a time of corporate downsizing. As a result, they learned not to trust corporations and institutions.

This environment taught them the importance of loyalty to a project — but, be aware, this group of workers is not necessarily loyal to a company.

What else characterizes this young cadre of workers? They:

- Are self reliant, flexible and adapt quickly to change
- Are fiercely independent, but express more satisfaction with their work than previous generations
- Are strong in multi-tasking, parallel thinking, and problem solving
- Think work should be fun and are not prone to work long hours, opting for a balance between work, family, and fun
- Want variety and options in their work and despise routine. (A quick way to lose up-and-coming Gen Xers is to pigeon-hole them in dead-end tasks, no matter how well executed.)

More than any previous generation, Gen Xers are motivated by money. They are equally motivated by the opportunity for new experiences, expanded responsibility, training, and the chance to master new technology.

This is the first group of employees to grow up with computers. State-of-the-art hardware, software, and related training are musts for this generation.

Gen Xers also want:

- Marketable skills
- Relationships with decision-makers
- Creative challenges
- Growing spheres of responsibility
- Opportunities for creative expression
- Control over their schedules
- Teams with clear goals and roles
- Leadership that is facilitative

One important caveat: Do not communicate with Gen Xers by memo. Whenever possible, contact should be face-to-face. With this personal interaction, you remove the institutional feel so undesirable to this important group of employees.

Child-centered parenting. In the early nineties, parents moved the spotlight back from themselves to their children. The eighties, the so called 'me' decade, had passed and as has been the pattern over the last century the pendulum swung back strongly in the other direction. No longer left behind while their parents traveled, kids explored the world with them…. even Las Vegas became family friendly. Not since the early sixties when boomers were kids was interest so focused on children.

The results have been mixed. Millennials typically have good relationships with their parents, even considering them close friends. Unfortunately, their parents tended to coddle their children, keeping their lives free from pain, fear, and disappointments. For instance, I know of one mother who completely filled out her son's college applications, including essays. Most of us from earlier generations cringe at this thought, but it is more common today than you might think. As a consequence of this parenting style, Millennials often have trouble adjusting to life without Mom and Dad. Where Generation X led the movement back into urban living, Millennials are not in a hurry to get out from under their parents' roofs.

> *Not since the early sixties when boomers were kids was interest so focused on children.*

Their close relationship with parents has made them more comfortable and casual around adults. A couple of years ago, I took one of my team's sharp young Millennials to a client meeting. It was one of those meetings you are familiar with. The client was relatively new and it was early in the project where we were just beginning to build their confidence in our ability to solve their problem. When the client asked him a question during the meeting, he confidently began his response with the phrase "Dude…" I was shocked, and so was the client. The young engineer, however, was oblivious. After later explaining to this young man that this type of language does not promote the professional image necessary to build the level of trust required to succeed as a consultant, he gladly never used that language again with a client.

This example, however, does address the comfort level and casualness they feel around adults. It also highlights one area— client interaction— where we as their mentors and managers must help them grow.

About two years ago, I had a 19-year-old intern, who had been with us only about two months, walk into my office one day while I was doing paperwork and just start looking around, browsing books on the shelves, and reading the certificates on the wall. After a few moments, I raised my head up from my desk to ask if I could help him with anything. "No", he replied. "I was just wondering what the heck it is you do?" Can you imagine even walking into your boss' office when you were a young intern? It was akin to being called to the principal's office in school. You avoided it like the plague. Yet this young man was not intimidated at all.

> *They just relate to older adults differently than we did, mostly because of the nature of the relationship with their parents.*

In my travels, I've often had design firm principals complain that these examples demonstrate a clear disrespect for their elders. After working with them for a number of years now, I don't think this is the case. They just relate to older adults differently than we did, mostly because of the nature of the relationship with their parents. The way respect is expressed is first learned at home. Parents spending the majority of their time with their children, volunteering at school, coaching every sport league, etc., and emphasizing the friendship aspect of their relationship have reared children who want to be their mentors friend. They really don't intend to come off as disrespectful. Instead, they engage with their elders as they would their peers. So, don't take it personal. In fact, the young man who came into my office has turned out to be a superstar performer with tremendous prospects for a long and successful engineering career. He graduates soon and we are working diligently to bring him on board.

Parent advocacy. Not only did parents center their lives around their children, and schedule their every minute, they also put them in a protective cocoon. Teachers today are not allowed to give too many poor grades, and certainly are discouraged from ever holding back a student. Bad grades often lead to parent/teacher conferences where the teacher is on trial. When I was in school, my parents always assumed the teacher was right. No more. Today's teachers have to battle not only the students, but the parents as well.

In her book *Moppets With Helmets,* Hara Estroff Marono says today's parenting equation is "life minus feeling bad equals a shot at happiness...the development needs of the young are subordinated to the psychological needs of adults."

Today, there's a new term called "helicopter parents," defined in Wikipedia as "a person who pays extremely close attention to his or her child or children, particularly at educational institutions. They rush to prevent any harm or failure from befalling them or letting them learn from their own mistakes, sometimes even contrary to the children's wishes. They are so named because, like a helicopter, they hover closely overhead, rarely out of reach whether their children need them or not. In Scandinavia, this phenomenon is known as 'curling parenthood'— describing parents who sweep all obstacles off ahead of their children." Colleges

> *"Life minus feeling bad equals a shot at happiness...the development needs of the young are subordinated to the psychological needs of adults."*

today are wrestling with how to get these parents to stay off of their campuses.

I actually had one architectural principal in Florida tell me one candidate's mother showed up at the interview with him! They chose not to interview the candidate…which was probably a wise decision. I've read many similar stories on the internet of parents calling to complain about their child's negative performance evaluations. I can't imagine personally experiencing this in the office, but it's probably coming. Perhaps it's only an indictment against the parents and not the kids. However, there is certainly some retraining required.

It often bothers me our society's parents have become so protective. We never wore bicycle helmets as children, nor did we have to sit in a car seat until we were eight years old! These are the kids whose mothers first put the "Caution, Baby on Board" signs in the back of their windows. Sometimes, I wonder how far our society will let it go. I've always been a personal believer in "what doesn't kill you makes you stronger. It builds character."

My wife, however, reminded me of why parents have been somewhat forced in this direction. When I was a child, I rode my bicycle two miles through a neighborhood and wooded areas to elementary school, along with my siblings and classmates. Today, you are hesitant to let your child walk down the street to a neighbor's house. Why? Our society, either real or perceived, is no longer as safe. With a barrage of news stories of child abductions, child molesters, and child murderers, parents are compelled to watch their children closer, especially on the internet where child predators can operate in relative anonymity.

> *I actually had one architectural principal in Florida tell me one candidate's mother showed up at the interview with him!*

Busy, busy, busy. The Millennials have been the busiest generation North America has ever seen, facing pressure levels normally only seen by adults. Parents, as well as teachers, have micromanaged their schedules, leaving little if any unstructured free time. From Little League baseball, to Pee Wee football, to soccer, swim team, and the like, sports seasons are never ending. Some of my friends have their nine-year-old boys in regular baseball throughout the spring and summer and then travel to various states with teams the rest of the year for weekend tournaments.

I recently took five of the youngest Millennials on our team to lunch and asked questions about some of their generation's characteristics. Were they accurate and where did they come from? When mentioning this particular characteristic, I asked why they did not rebel and demand more unstructured time to play with their friends. Problem was, according to them, since there friends were also in these activities, this was the only chance to spend time with them. I would not have figured that out on my own.

> *Popular parenting magazines have emphasized overindulging your kids in multiple activities to keep them well rounded and prepared for college.*

My wife, who is very perceptive of the influences of pop culture, has said for years the popular parenting magazines have emphasized overindulging your kids in multiple activities to keep them well-rounded and prepared for college. Parents have bought into these philosophies and transformed the traditional 'soccer mom' into two parents running a taxi cab service driving their kids from one activity to the next, pushing them to excel.

The size of the Millennial generation has accentuated this trend. Since the demand for admittance into our nation's colleges and universities has rapidly exceeded the supply of available seats, the entrance requirements have greatly increased. Today, college preparation begins in sixth grade, and often sooner, with a focus on being competitive. Kids are pressured to do volunteer work, take advanced classes, and add as many extra-curricular activities they can to pad their college applications. Many even take on-campus college classes their senior year in high school.

Multiculturalism. Millennials grew up in a world rich in ethnicity and diversity. Tolerance of both race and religion were stressed throughout their educative years. Recent data from UCLA's Higher Education Research Institute shows that interracial interaction among college freshmen has reached a record high.

Fear. While young, most Millennials witnessed the bombing of the Murrah federal building in Oklahoma City, the Columbine High School shooting, and ultimately, the terrorist attacks on September 11th, 2001. While we grew up under the threat of total annihilation during the Cold War, theirs was a much more intimate perspective. They were the first students to walk through metal detectors to enter high schools patrolled by armed officers and never knew the experience of walking up to the arrival gate in an airport to welcome a visiting relative.

"They know the way things go down and are no longer naïve about the workings of the world and the intentions of businesses and other organizations."

— Peter Sheahan, *Generation Y: Thriving and Surviving with Generation Y at Work.*

Globalism. Millennials are the first to enter a globally competitive environment. In his book, *The World is Flat*, author Thomas Friedman quotes Bill Gates as observing that if in the 1960s and 1970s you compared the opportunities for success of an average student in Cincinnati, Ohio with that of an extremely talented student in rural India, odds greatly favored the average student. Today, Gates noted, this is no longer the case. The best ideas and talent rise to the top, with fewer limitations based on geography.

Today's generation is often more in touch with the world around them, as the internet has made communicating globally immensely easier and, of course, free.

DEFINING CHARACTERISTICS

I hesitate to list characteristics Millennials share for just as with any generation there are few representatives that would demonstrate every trait exactly. However, it is a helpful way to understand how they think as a group. So what traits do they share in common? What are their dreams and what motivates them? What type of firms would they most likely be attracted to and want to make their home? Here are some of the common themes that, if we understand them, can give us an edge in creating the right culture and management style for Millennials:

College graduates are now encouraged by many organizations to take on teaching assignments in tough, inner city schools as a way to give back. These programs are very popular. A professor friend of mine was very dismayed when his son, a senior in college, announced he was going to delay his pursuit of a graduate degree so he could teach math in the inner city. After arguing, his son reminded both parents that they had always encouraged him to give back to his community. Three years later, after helping a team turn a Washington, D.C. high school's test scores from worst to first; he did enter a law program.

In her book, *Connecting Generations: The Sourcebook*, Claire Raines defined several messages prevalent from Millennials' parents and teachers that subconsciously helped shape and mold their thinking:

- **Be smart, you are special.** They've been catered to since they were tiny. Think Nickelodeon, Baby Gap, and *Sports Illustrated for Kids.*

- **Leave no one behind.** They were taught to be inclusive and tolerant of other races, religions, and sexual orientations.

- **Connect 24/7.** They learned to be interdependent on family, friends, and teachers. More Millennials say they can live without the television than the computer. Many prefer chatting online to talking on the phone.

- **Achieve now!** Some parents hired private agents to line up the right college; others got started choosing the right preschool while the child was still in the womb.
- **Serve your community.** Fifty percent of high school students reported volunteering in their communities, many of their high schools requiring community service hours for graduation. On one Roper survey, when Millennials were asked for the major cause of problems in the U.S., they answered *selfishness.*

Where we had this burning desire to plow through school and get it done so we could get on with our career and life, Millennials are not in such a hurry.

Work/life balance. Even though they were busy as children, and perhaps because of it, Millennials place a high priority on achieving and maintaining what they see as a proper work/life balance, seeking to balance the pursuit of a career with family and play. They are often willing to take less pay, even delay the start of their careers in order to achieve some of the other goals in their lives.

Our firm recently completed a survey of engineering students in their sophomore and junior years asking them to rank a list of 15 different incentives upon which they would consider signing on early with us. The goal was to figure out an offer package that would take the talented candidates off the market before other firms began pursuing them. The top three results were not surprising. Salary, benefits, and career opportunities were one, two, and three. We did, however, leave room on the bottom of the survey for other ideas not mentioned. The one that came up quite frequently was a desire to delay the start date for some period after graduation. A number of candidates explained that the ability to have a job secured but yet be able to delay starting work until a few months after graduation would be considered a significant benefit to them. I found that interesting, and in reality, it did not cost us anything to offer this benefit.

> *They are often willing to take less pay, even delay the start of their careers in order to achieve some of the other goals in their lives.*

Confidence bordering on cockiness. Raised by parents, teachers, and athletic coaches who focused on the importance of self-esteem, they enter the workforce ready to tackle any challenge. Problem is, they do not have enough work experience to properly do so. A few weeks ago, one of my Gen X leaders had a new civil engineering graduate join his team. After a week of having his offers to help further explain tasks ignored, he told this Millennial, "We don't expect you to know anything about what we do when you graduate, and that's OK. It takes time to learn." You know this to be true! Most architects and engineers come out of college knowing little about how to put together a set of plans or specifications for even the smallest project. Instead, they only have the tools necessary to begin integrating with practical experience.

This can be problematic in our business. While we certainly want young people who desire to grow in their field and gradually take on more responsibility, taking on more than they can handle early on can lead to disaster for a firm.

"…Boomers have given them the confidence to be optimistic about their ability to make things happen, and Xers have given them just enough skepticism to be cautious…If you want to remember just one key word to describe Millennials, it's realistic."

— Lynne C. Lancaster and David Stillman
When Generations Collide.

Optimistic with high expectations. They are optimistic about the future, but not in an impractical way. They do have high expectations, often spurred on by stories of how Google, a company filled to the brim with Millennials, treats its employees. On-site gymnasiums and massage therapists, casual dress codes, flexible hours, telecommuting, free food, and the like are some of the stories their web friends share.

The stories of Google's culture are legendary. While we can never compete with that kind of atmosphere, it is necessary to understand this is the Millennials' gold standard our firm's culture, salary, and benefits are being measured against.

Focus on achievement. Millennial parents drove their children in pursuit of success even before they left the womb. When I went to first grade, they taught you how to read. Today, children are expected to be readers before they enter kindergarten. Their mothers, whose average age is higher than any generation in history, often put flourishing careers on hold to stay home with their children. The drive and energy that went into a career was redirected towards child-rearing.

College prep began at an early age with pressure to learn a foreign language (they now teach Spanish in first grade), compete in multiple sports, learn music and taekwondo. To pad a college resume, be well-rounded, or whatever the goal, achievement was the focus.

As a result, Millennials like a feeling of achievement, but are not used to having to set their own goals. Parents, teachers, and coaches did all the goal-setting for them. They are, however, very intelligent, especially those that can survive architectural or engineering school. A founder of a 25-year-old, 60-person engineering firm in the Northwest noted this was the first generation he had meet that could actually write a business letter upon graduation.

Difficulty with criticism. My daughters, both of whom are Millennials, entered into soccer at the same time, and on the same team. Unfortunately, their team did not have the best talent in the league. In fact, they did not win a game all season. However, it did not matter too much because the league did not keep score. Why? Because "winning and losing does not matter," I was told. "We want to focus on strong self-esteem."

Sounds good, I guess, but the problem is, in business, there are often winners and losers. Also, in order to excel, you have to be willing to receive constructive criticism from bosses and peers in order to grow. The cocoon of protection in which Millennials were raised has left them inexperienced in receiving criticism, especially when it is direct.

A desire to be green. From an early age, Millennials have been bombarded with "Save The Planet" messages. Whether on television or in the classroom, this message was continually reinforced. As a result, they are very sensitive to actions that are environmentally friendly. A recent newspaper article on where Millennials live interviewed three different Millennial architectural interns. Some of their comments were "Green design is a trend the way indoor plumbing is a trend. Seriously, today's 20-somethings

> *Being green is just a way of life. It's so important, I wouldn't date someone who didn't recycle.*

are more globally aware and civic-minded than tuned-out and cynical Generation X. Being green is just a way of life. It's so important, I wouldn't date someone who didn't recycle."

Wanting to be in smaller, more environmentally friendly houses than their parents McMansions, most of their personal decisions are influenced by its impact on the environment. Knowing your carbon footprint, whether individual or corporate, is important to them.

A desire to give back. Millennials have ran from the 'me' generation of the 1980s in a way not seen since Boomers first entered the Peace Corps en masse. Summer vacations often involve trips to Third World countries to help give back through medical or building missions.

A recent *USA Today* article noted significant spikes in the number of applications and projected enrollment of freshman classes at colleges and universities in New Orleans. Why? In response to Hurricane Katrina, the city is the place to go for young volunteers who want to put a battered community back together. There is a sense within Millennials of making the world a better place. Sal Liberto, Loyola's vice president for enrollment said "students know they're coming down to have an adventure. It's a great time to be part of something…the rebirth of a city."

Technology is in their blood. The Veterans generation has mostly ignored technology while Boomers have reluctantly accepted its invasion on society. Gen Xers embraced technology, but Millennials can't imagine life without it. If you want to get a "this guy's older than dirt" look, try to describe the old punch cards that preceded floppy disks. In fact, talk about floppy disks themselves.

According to Jeff VanKooten, senior consultant with the Colorado-based Center for Generational Studies "You and I are immigrants to (Millennials') world. They are the natives of technology. They're the indigenous (peoples) when it comes to technology, and we need to tap into that and be humble enough to give up that form of control."

This generation grew up in the height of the electronic gaming craze, learning how to live and connect in virtual worlds. Having a cell phone with instant messaging, Internet access, music and video files is a must to be normal.

It has changed how education works as well. Computer class begins at an early age, and homework research is done online. Recently, my fifth-grade son came to me with a crisis. Our internet connection was down and he could not look up his vocabulary definitions. I responded, "Just use the dictionary." He had no idea what I meant. After beating him handily in a game of checkers on our last vacation, he commented observantly that I was better at 'old-fashioned' games like checkers and he was better at 'new' games like his Nintendo Wii. He's got that right!

They're the indigenous (peoples) when it comes to technology, and we need to tap into that and be humble enough to give up that form of control.

On a side note, I have found technology has helped me manage him better as a student. Like me, at that age, I loathed doing homework and often did not accurately describe all my pending assignments to my parents. With him,

I can just go to www.schoolnotes.com where his assignments are posted by teacher, or email his teacher direct to verify his story. Needless to say, I'm glad my parents did not have these tools when I was in the sixth grade.

In their recent book, *Connecting to the Net Generation*, Reynol Junco and Jeanna Mastrodicasa found that in a survey of 7,705 college students in the US:

- 97% own a computer
- 94% own a cell phone
- 76% use instant messaging.
- 15% of IM users are logged on 24 hours a day/7 days a week
- 34% use web sites as their primary source of news
- 28% author a blog and 44% read blogs
- 49% download music using peer-to-peer file sharing
- 75% of college students have a Facebook account
- 60% own some type of portable music and/or video device such as an iPod.

Millennials use the internet exclusively to do research. We never have a potential Millennial candidate interview with us that has not thoroughly researched the firm in advance through our web site. Recently, we hired the valedictorian of a reputable school's engineering class who had competing offers from many other firms. Before accepting our offer, however, he voiced concern about our web site. "What do you mean", I inquired. "We have a very nice web site." Yet, according to him, our web site was out of date and reflected a company who was not up to speed with the times. He was right, of course. Our web site had not been worked on in over six years when we gave it the last major overhaul. However, to this day, I can't figure out what it is about our site that signals it's 'out of date'. I guess if you spend a large majority of your time on the web then it is intuitively obvious.

Peer-oriented. Millennials are well-connected to their peers, who may just as likely be on the other side of the world as next door. They like integrating with large groups and often prefer online communication to one-on-one. One of their favorite means of communicating is blogging in the blogosphere. For those of us less technically minded individuals, blogging is an open forum online to provide opinions, or vent, about subjects as varied as proper maintenance of a 1957 Chevy carburetor to theories on space travel. Often, larger A/E firms are discussed, dissected, and laid bare in the blogosphere.

Seek instant gratification. Not that this is new to Millennials. The world has been speeding up ever since the Industrial Revolution took place. The amount of time required to do basic tasks, travel, and communicate over long distances has been shrinking for years. The Information Revolution, however, has exponentially increased this compaction of time. To Millennials, even e-mail is 'old school'. They prefer 'instant' messaging. They grew up in a world with ever increasing computer processing speeds allowing instant downloads and file sharing.

While working on this chapter on a recent flight, I sat next to a Millennial. As soon as it was safe to use electronic devices, out came his iPhone and headset. On that tiny device he enjoyed a movie throughout the flight. It's hard for me to imagine growing up without having to entertain oneself by counting cows along the highway on road trips, playing the alphabet game with billboard signs, or seeing how many different state license plates you could identify. Anything to pass the hours. Today, parents just pop in one video after another.

How the Age Bubble Is Transforming the Workplace— and What You Can Do to Prepare

Six years ago, the increasing workforce shortage problem was already readily apparent. The demographics of the workforce are undergoing a dramatic change. Even in 2002, 11 percent of the active work force was already over 56 years old, a percentage that has steadily grown as Baby Boomers aged. Organizations —including design firms—are already being warned to prepare for the steady departure of huge numbers of their most experienced people.

So, what was some of the advice being given to help firms prepare for the generational shift in the work force? At that time, Bruce Tulgan at RainMakerThinking® (*www.rainmakerthinking.com*), a consultant on young people in the workplace, gave five key tactics which are still applicable today:

1. Forestall the retirement of as many older workers as possible. Whenever feasible, support semi-retirement through flexible work arrangements: flexible schedules, telecommuting, and flexible conditions of employment. Build giant reserve armies of retirees. Immediately begin the process of capturing and transferring the knowledge, skill, and wisdom of older workers. This could involve building an online knowledge archive.

2. Call upon Boomers to resume their youthful role as change leaders. Now is the time to abandon hierarchical norms, sink-or-swim management, and one-size-fits-all career paths.

3. Prepare Gen Xers for supervisory responsibility and leadership roles. Gen Xers are now entering their prime working years in short supply and full of attitude. Xers want status, authority, and rewards, but often resist traditional management roles. Create new paths to leadership, redesign leadership roles, and develop the new generation of leaders for those roles.

4. Accelerate the professional development of Millennial employees. Recruit new employees at younger ages, get them up to speed faster, and trust them with important roles involving critical tasks and responsibilities. There's no choice; there won't be enough older experienced workers to get all the work done. Teach managers to coach these high-maintenance younger workers every step of the way on every single thing—from time management to customer service.

5. Be prepared to exert more pressure to get more and better work out of fewer people. Everyone will have to work smarter, faster, better, and probably longer and harder, too. Highly skilled, hands-on, coaching-style management will still be the key to success.

CHAPTER 2

Power Shift

"Kids, I don't know what's wrong with the kids today."
– From Bye Bye Birdie

Now that we have described who Millennials are, a reasonable place to begin is with the question "Why should we change our workplaces for them?"

Let's begin with a mental exercise for Boomers and Early Generation Xers, those of us born before 1978. Let your thoughts wander back for a moment to your first experience working for a design firm. What was the office atmosphere like? Did you punch a time card? Sit behind a drafting table? Was smoking allowed anywhere in the office? Were you required to wear a tie every day? Were there very many, if any, female professionals in the office?

Take the exercise even further. What was your first boss like? Did he wear a three-piece suit each day? Did he take much time to socialize with the new hires or share feedback and constructive input on your performance?

How about your interview process? Were you wined and dined, with most of the time together spent with your interviewers touting the many reasons why their firm would be an excellent choice for your career and family, or was the whole process about you selling yourself?.

And what did the entrenched generation think about us? Did they think we were as committed to the job as they were? Did they make fun of your lettering on the drafting table, lamenting the good old days when lettering was a beautiful art form?

It's safe to say that those old codgers would have been shocked and maybe even dismayed to see where we took the industry. Yet, it survives and thrives. Some of us young whippersnappers are now leading firms larger than our old bosses could have ever dreamed, serving clients across the globe and delivering projects at a pace that would have then been unimaginable.

There have certainly been some structural changes to our entire industry that have drastically modified the way in which we delivery our services. Computer-aided design (CAD), for one, has rendered traditional drafting obsolete, while creating new issues related to intellectual property. The advent of the fax machine, then e-mail, cell phones, Blackberries, etc., have compressed the window of time in which our clients expect a response, and eaten away at time allowed for design and construction. Today, encroaching trends such as building information modeling, globalization, and outsourcing will further modify our industry's structure even more than CAD and in ways that we cannot fully anticipate.

> *It's safe to say that those old codgers would have been shocked and maybe even dismayed to see where we took the industry.*

FAST FORWARD

"I'm not changing for them!" bemoans a 45-year-old Washington, D.C.-based engineering firm principal to me recently, at the suggestion of offering a more flexible schedule to accommodate the requests of his Millennial staff. "When I came into this business, nobody asked me what I wanted. I was expected to abide by the rules and work hard," he continues. "Kids out of college these days don't respect the value of hard work and paying your dues."

Does he have a point? Maybe, but the team of engineers which he is responsible for has turnover rates equal to twice our industry's average, and is even higher with his younger employees. The real question should be what impact this high turnover rate has on his bottom line. A recent survey of design firm CEOs suggested costs ranging from $15,000 to $75,000 per lost employee, as shown in Table 1-1. My personal experience suggests even the high end of these numbers are low because they do not fully account for the "opportunity costs," which is the lost potential revenue (and profit) that would have been generated if the team member had stayed.

Table 1-1
Cost of Employee Turnover

CFO Responses*	$ per Employee	What Makes Up the Cost
Lowest 10% of CFO respondents	$5,000	Recruiting fees, training expenses, management interviewing time, human resource time, advertising, severance
Lowest 25% of CFO respondents	$15,000	
Median	$30,000	All items in the previous group, plus lost revenue, lost productivity, initial inefficiency, relocation fees
Highest 25% of CFO respondents	$50,000	All items in the previous groups, plus additional salary for new employees (generally higher than worker lost), lost clients, damaged client relations, rework on projects, lost knowledge
Highest 10% of CFO respondents	$75,000	
* Responses by 110 chief financial officers of engineering and construction firms in 2006 survey conducted by EFCG Inc.		

Two years ago, one of my star Millennials walked into my office and asked if we could talk (always gives you a bad feeling in your gut when this happens, doesn't it?). He told me that, although he loved working on our team, he had decided to leave engineering to become a financial planner. What could I say? I knew he was sharp enough to succeed in any type of business. Over the next year, however, I was constantly reminded of what his decision to leave cost our team when project opportunities arose which we could have easily pursued and profitably delivered if he had stayed. Today, he would have been a registered engineer with unlimited potential. How do you even attempt to account for that cost?

While there are reasons great employees leave that are beyond our control, such as a career change, or the need to relocate for family reasons, most of the turnover that occurs in our design firms is preventable. There's no use sweating about the ones we can't control, but there is much to be gained by focusing on the ones we can. I'm often reminded of The Serenity Prayer: "God grant me the serenity to accept the things I cannot change; courage to change the things I can; and wisdom to know the difference."

TIMES ARE CHANGING

Of all the changes since our careers began, the power shift that has occurred over the past 10 years in the employee/employer relationship is one of the most subtle, yet powerful of all. In this time period, the design industry has moved from being an employer-leveraged industry to an employee-leveraged industry, where it is the employee that truly has the upper hand.

To prove the point, think back again to your first interview. Did you spend a lot of time negotiating your offer package in terms of salary and benefits? Did you have three or more attractive offers from our industry in areas in which you were interested? Most likely not. If you were like me, you were just ecstatic to have a job and took whatever was offered. Remember how hard it was to land that first position? Everyone wanted only to hire someone with experience, but no one wanted to provide that experience. The old *catch-22*. Back then, if you didn't know somebody that could help you get into the business, you were out of luck.

Source: *Handbook of Industrial & Organizational Psychology*

I've asked hundreds of design firm principals these questions about their early work experience. After pondering the past, with a slight smile on their face, they bring up similar memories, long since buried. Interestingly enough, the phrase I most consistently hear when describing the first firm they first worked for is "sweat shop." Most remember the boss with an office behind glass carefully located so they could monitor a large production floor of tightly packed rows of drafting tables. Most spent all of there early years focused on menial tasks, never leaving the office to participate in client meetings or participate in firm marketing or planning. Rather just small cogs in a production machine.

How things have changed. Today, if you have not approached a candidate well before their last semester of college begins, you're probably too late. I can't remember the last time I interviewed a soon-to-be newly minted engineer that did not have offers pending from at least two of our direct competitors.

It's always been about supply and demand, but the demand for architects, engineers, interior designers, scientists, and surveyors in our business has grown consistently while the supply of potential candidates continually shrinks. Table 1-2 shows the number of architects and engineers graduating from US institutions peaked in the mid-80s. What's not shown is the impact of greater numbers of these graduates choosing other career paths upon graduation. New architectural graduates often pursue career paths in computer animation, CGI, and other graphical computer-related careers, working for Disney, Lucasfilm, or Electronic Arts. In the late 90s, many engineering graduates were lured with lucrative offers by technology, internet, and telecommunication firms at the height of the dot-com boom. Compounding the problem, we now have the largest generation ever in the workforce, Boomers, entering retirement age and we have not created the "supply" needed to match demand.

> *I can't remember the last time I interviewed a soon-to-be newly minted engineer that did not have offers pending from at least two of our direct competitors.*

We, as A/E firm leaders, however, are not alone in this struggle. Today, while flying across the country, I sat next to the CEO of a large regional bank based in Oklahoma and Texas. According to him, the banking industry did little in terms of recruiting over the past 20 years. Now, with

Boomers rapidly retiring, bankers are investing significant effort in figuring out how to attract Millennials to their industry. In fact, he has a team of people recruiting at the high school level. Good news is, we are not the only industry struggling with a workforce shortage. Bad news, we are competing against them all for Millennials.

Table 1-2
Bachelor Degrees Awarded

WHERE DID THEY ALL GO?

So what happened to our supply chain of human resources? Why did the numbers of graduates shrink in the first place and why did our very respectable profession become less attractive? Unfortunately, current design firm professionals, and our predecessors, created the environment that led to the problem, especially in the area of salaries. Over the past 20 years, as shown in Figure 1-3, salaries in our industry have not kept pace with inflation!

For instance, a recent study of the top 100 salaries in the United States ranked civil engineers number 67, only one ahead of art directors, and architects, number 82, just one notch ahead of administrative service managers. Now, from a pure financial analysis, what's the return on investment for our efforts? Do the typical art degree program entrance requirements demand the same GPA and SAT scores required to get into a good architectural or engineering program? Is an art student required to put the same level of effort necessary to survive freshman chemistry, years of calculus, or all-nighters in the design studio? When I was in college, the art students started partying on Thursday nights to get a jump on the weekend.

Table 1-3
A/E Salary Growth

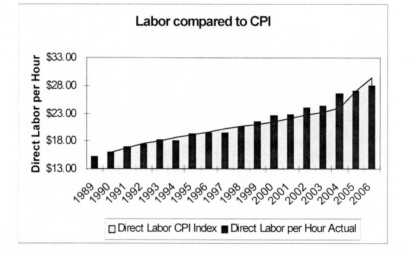

How about risk? Does an art director deal in designs that could kill people? Is the fee they can obtain on a project assignment dwarfed in comparison with the potential liability?

Scottish businessman Sir Fraser Morrison, who along with his son Peter just acquired Hillier Architecture under their Scottish-based firm RMJM to become the world's seventh-largest architectural firm, was quoted in an article in the June 2008 edition of the magazine *ARCHITECT* said, "First and foremost, the financial reward for architects is 'minuscule'; so that the agent who sells a building will often earn a higher fee than the firm that designed it." Morrison certainly has a point here. An A/E team designs a new office building for fees often as low as 4% to 5% of total construction value. How much does a realtor get to sell the building? Usually in the neighborhood of 6%. How many times can we normally be paid to design the building versus how many times a realtor can sell the building? For that matter, how many years of higher education were required to get that realtor's license?

Table 1-4
Starting Salary Comparison
From PSMJ's *2008 A/E Management Salary Survey*

Starting Salaries of Engineers

The Morrisons go on to ponder, "…why a top-tier design firm can't command the same respect and compensation for its 'intellectual capital' as McKinsey, the famed management consultant firm does." As two businessmen without design professional backgrounds, they have been able to take an outsider's view of our industry and see much room for improvement from a business standpoint.

But we architects and engineers are ethical professionals. We tend to view charging our beloved clients anything beyond fees with minuscule profit margins to be akin to robbery. As a result, we constantly fight to hold down salaries and benefits, which are usually 75% of our total cost of operations.

The point is finding candidates is getting increasingly difficult, and there is no reason to believe it will not continue to do so over the next 10 years. Unlike cyclical work slowdowns in the past, the next design impacted recession is only likely to make workloads more manageable instead of leading to mass layoffs as we have often seen before. To reiterate, over the past 10 years, our industry has transitioned from an employer-leveraged industry, where the firm held all the power, to an employee-leveraged industry, where employees now call the shots. In addition, all of the data suggest this transition is going to continue well into the foreseeable future. In their recently published book *When Professionals Have to Lead*, authors Thomas Delong, John Gabarro, and Robert Lees confirm this is the case not only for professional design firms, but for all professional service firms. In the book, they make a strong case for the need for a new leadership model that focuses specifically on attracting and retaining professionals.

> *Over the past 10 years, our industry has transitioned from an employer-leveraged industry, where the firm held all the power, to an employee-leveraged industry, where employees now call the shots.*

As an example, Figure 1-5 shows the results of surveys of design firm CEOs over the past three years. In each of these years, design firm leaders say it has become increasingly difficult to find staff and, at the more senior levels, it is next to impossible. In fact, for the first time this past year, 100% of firm leaders ranked senior professionals and project managers as difficult to find. As a result, to grow your firm or even to maintain current staffing levels over time, your only reasonable choice is to attract, retain, and empower Millenials in your organization, but how?

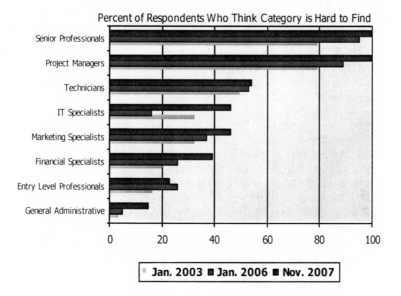

Figure 1-5: Finding Potential Employees

Workforce Shortage: A Challenge for Rainmakers

Most A/E firms are acutely aware that they are facing a long-term shortage of labor in the technical fields. Who will do the work rainmakers bring in, and where will the future leaders and rainmakers come from?

Kay C. Godwin, principal of Marketing Avenues, and Karen W. Winters, principal of AEC Marketing Insights, addressed this problem in their white paper for the SMPS Foundation, titled *The Looming A/E/C Workforce Shortage*. Their paper focused on recruiting and retention strategies adopted by AEC firms and other industries to solve workforce shortage issues. It contains more than 75 specific strategies that organizations are using to recruit and retain their best employees.

Because marketers are so familiar with the process of selling intangibles, they should participate in developing recruiting strategies for their firms. Kay and Karen outlined in their paper the strategies that some firms are using to mitigate the effects of this shortage.

Mentoring to interns. A number of A/E firms offer internships and mentoring as part of their recruiting program. For example, EDAW, the San Francisco-based landscape architecture and community planning services firm, hosts the EDAW Summer Student Program, enabling it to recruit top students worldwide. The program involves students in a two-week charrette-style workshop addressing real project issues. The workshop is followed by a paid eight-week office internship.

Reach out to Millennials. The University of Illinois College of Engineering shared ideas for recruiting college graduates. Because Millennials value rich experiences and work/life balance, companies should bring them into their offices to experience the feel and chemistry of the work environment and to highlight the collaborative and social aspects of the company culture.

Building employee commitment is the key to retention. It requires that employees have a sense of belonging; understand the mission, vision, and strategy communicated by the firm's leaders; and develop trust and respect for their managers. A variety of retention strategies can help achieve this goal.

Train managers. Given the importance of managers in building employee commitment, firms should provide training and mentoring for new managers to increase their people skills.

Create collaborative, diverse teams. Small firms in our industry tend to work collaboratively simply because people have to be generalists and "wear different hats" in order to accomplish the work. In larger firms, however, people often separate into disciplinary or departmental silos, making it a challenge to develop collaborative teams who can focus together on a particular client group or set of issues.

Initiate employee development programs. Professional development programs are key to creating committed employees. The building and development company, Gilbane, implemented an informal program called Career Conversations in which employees are encouraged to meet with their supervisors to discuss career growth and enhancement. Gilbane's HR director credits this program for improving employee retention by 40%.

California-based construction firm Swinerton Inc. offers a leadership program designed to teach team dynamics, the role of a leader, difficult conversations, hiring right, and case study work.

Entice older employees to stay. Like a number of other organizations, Flad & Associates is enlisting older workers to act as mentors for the younger staff. The firm has also instituted much more flexibility into the work schedule, and is keeping older workers by offering part-time or other project work.

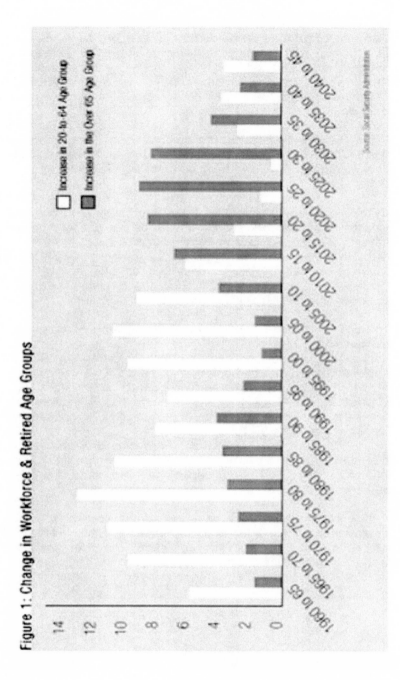

Figure 1: Change in Workforce & Retired Age Groups

CHAPTER 3

It's Your Culture, Stupid

"Don't be a Cake Eater."
— Young civil engineer offering advice on
how sell our firm to Millennials.
(explanation for Boomers and Gen Xers to follow)

In the 1992 election, James Carville, Bill Clinton's chief political strategist, got a wavering campaign back on track by shouting "It's the economy, stupid." This refrain helped Clinton, and his allies, realize the economy was people's number-one concern and focusing primarily on this issue could win the election. In 1996, Clinton repeated the lesson learned by asking the same question at campaign stop after campaign stop: "Are you better off today financially than you were four years ago?"

In the battle to attract, retain, and empower Millennials, nothing can take the place of having the right culture. My team has had offers accepted from new graduates recently that had other offers from direct competitors, often for more money or with signing bonuses. When we inquire as to why, the answers always relate to our culture. Earlier today, an architect friend of mine in Louisiana shared this story:

"We just hired a new Millennial yesterday. She turned down a half-dozen more lucrative offers with bigger firms. When I asked why she did that, she said our firm was the firm of the future and she loved her interview with the entire office. She told me she would sit on the floor and work, or work in an unconditioned barn if we didn't have a seat for her in our 1,000 square foot office with 12 people."

Now that's a firm that is doing something right.

WHAT CULTURE DO MILLENIALS WANT?

Perhaps the best way to find out what Millennials believe to be the ideal workplace is to hear it directly from them. The following is from a blog (that's what Millennials do) by Ryan Healy, founder of Brazen Careerist, an online community and career center for Millennials. Ryan, himself a Millennial, is a leading voice for his generation and gave me permission to reprint his article.

Now let me warn you before you begin. The material you are about to read may make your blood boil to the point you want to toss this book out the window. Before you do, understand this is what Millennials dream to be the IDEAL workplace. Not that one exists. However, the spirit of the message provides many clues we can apply to our own firm's culture.

7 Things to Look Past When Managing Millennials
by Ryan Healy

Managing Millennials isn't all that different from managing anyone else. You need to demand a lot, manage a lot, and respect the fact that they have a life outside of work. That being said, there are some things that Millennial employees believe that past generations may not have thought at the same age. So, for all you confused managers out there, here's a list of things you should consider accepting when it comes to managing Millennials.

*1. **What time he comes to work.** Sometimes I come to work at 7 a.m. Sometimes I come to work at 11 a.m. Sometimes I'll find myself all alone at the office for the better part of a day because my Millennial co-workers are somewhere else. Lucky for us, we work at a start up where we only care about face time if there is an important meeting. I don't mind if no one is at the office because I know that sometimes when I come in at 7 a.m., I have a hard time concentrating and get no work done. And sometimes when I come in at 11 a.m., I spent the entire morning in front of my laptop at home, getting a ton of work done.*

If you're managing a Millennial, and there are no important meetings on the schedule, don't worry about what time he comes to work. Because, as we all know, results matter. Hours don't.

2. What time he leaves work. *Yesterday I left work at 3 p.m. to take a nap. Today, I'll be working well past dinner. Maybe you got the point already, but I'll say it again, hours don't matter. Older folks can use the "I need to pick my kids up at school" excuse and walk out of work guilt-free. We twentysomethings aren't quite so lucky. You can only come up with so many doctor, dentist, and family emergency excuses before they are worn out.*

Create an environment where people don't judge ANYONE who decides to leave early on a sunny Friday afternoon to meet up with some friends, because everyone trusts that the work will be done come Monday morning.

3. What's on his computer screen? *Don't be surprised to see Facebook, Twitter, Brazen Careerist, ESPN, Gmail, Word, Excel, and Powerpoint all open at the same time on your Millennial's computer screen. In fact, only having those tabs open would be a fairly focused afternoon for me.*

But it's OK. We can still get our work done. All that stuff is open because, quite frankly, we're all a little ADD. Sending out a tweet or leaving a comment on a blog is a necessary distraction every 20 minutes or so. Honestly, lots of Millennials wonder how anyone can sit at a desk and do nothing but work for eight straight hours without going insane?

4. His ultimately meaningless fashion statements. *When I worked for IBM, I was on a project at the Pentagon. As you might guess, this required a full suit every single day. As if this wasn't painful enough, I swear my military co-workers shaved every hour on the hour. So when I walked in with my day-old stubble, I felt a little out of place.*

But you know what? I actually look better with a little stubble, and I would trade shaving for 10 extra minutes of sleep any day of the week. At one point, I decided to grow a goatee. I wanted to see when my boss would tell me to shave it. He told me to shave it after a week. I told him it was in style and kept it for another week.

The message is: you've got to look past a little facial hair, or a pair of open-toed sandals, and just worry about your employees' work ethic and production if you want to get the most out of them.

5. Anything he does at happy hour. *Everyone loves happy hour. It's the time to kick back, relax and unwind from a long day of work with the people you just worked with. Things happen. Drinks happen. We're all young, we're in our prime partying years, and some of us handle our liquor better than others. So whatever you do, don't judge your Millennial employees based on what happens toward the end of happy hour.*

The truth is, the managers should be long gone by the time things get a little crazy. And if they're not, they should be getting a little crazy, too. The worst thing I ever did at a happy hour (well, two hours after it officially ended) was engage in a little too much PDA with a co-worker. Not sure what came over us (hint: alcohol), and luckily no one saw it, but I can't imagine what would have happened if anyone did. My advice: ignore what happens at happy hours. If you can't, then I'd advise you stay away from the party.

6. His lack of "experience." *It's OK if your Millennial employee doesn't know how to punch a time clock and can't relate to your high school summer job experience. It has nothing to do with whether he will work hard for you. There is definite truth to the claim that you need to work hard as a child to learn the value of a dollar and the value of hard work, but what summer jobs can offer us is different now.*

Your Millennial overachiever couldn't have settled for a summer job at McDonald's if she wanted to, because a summer spent flipping burgers is not going to get you into Harvard. And it probably wouldn't get you into a lot of less competitive schools. But a summer spent volunteering in Africa will go a long way toward getting you into a good college, and it betters the world, too. Look past her lack of traditional experience, teach your Millennials how to do the little things that she's missed (even if you think it's stupid), and figure out how to capitalize on the knowledge and experience she gained from leading her business organization or studying abroad.

7. His personal phone calls. *When you were an entry-level worker, maybe you wouldn't have dreamed of calling your* *girlfriend to say hello right after lunch or dialing up your mechanic to schedule a time to drop your car off for service. But work and life are no longer two distinct entities and this goes for both the office and at home.*

Look past the fact that it's not business for everyone all the time at the office. Because just as I have no problem making personal calls at the office, I also have no problem making a business call or sending an e-mail during my "personal" hours in front of the TV. Life happens 24 hours a day and, now, so does work. So look past the personal phone calls at the office and enjoy how your Millennial worker will use the whole day to get those results you need for the business.

So, how's that blood-pressure doing? Yes, some of it is unreasonable and some is downright nuts. The online responses to this article have varied, mostly by generation. Millennials are very supportive, yet recognize some of these issues, such as flexible hours, are not conducive to every business. Boomers mostly responded in anger.

Before we can begin to review the potential cultural lessons from Ryan's article, we must first understand the key driver ingredient in any high performance organization's culture. Without it, achieving Ryan's vision of an ideal workplace and achieving our goals for our design firms will be impossible.

PUT THE FOCUS ON PERFORMANCE

When I first read Ryan's article, the most important message is high performance Millennials want you to focus on results and not hours. This is a powerful message! Most firms reward sacrifice over results, and I've never understood why. Perhaps it is simply because that's the way it has always been done. For years, design firm managers have been focusing on metrics such as utilization, the ratio of billable hours to non-billable hours, and the amount of overtime as the main measures of employee performance. However, studies such as the one in Figure 3-1 have shown there to be little correlation between profitability and utilization.

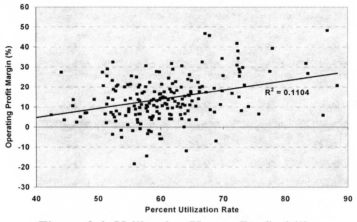

Figure 3-1: Utilization Versus Profitability

I personally understand their issue here. In my intern days, I worked very hard to be a producer and also put in the extra time needed to get the job done. I had a peer, however, who put in a lot more overtime because he had no life beyond the office. Since he was in no rush to leave, he was also in no rush to work diligently while in the office. As a result, he ended up producing less work than I even though he put in more hours. Unfortunately for me, the firm rewarded people based on overtime. How ridiculous, I thought at the time and still do to this day.

Overtime is an easy metric to track, but it is a poor indication of performance. The heart of Ryan Healy's message is, "Don't worry if I come in late or leave early, take a personal call in the afternoon, or look at a personal web site sometime during the day. Did I get the job done in an excellent manner? Am I driving the business?"

This summer, I found an A/E firm that does not give out vacation days. You just take as many as you want. Sound crazy? It sure does. However, the firm has found their people love the policy and end up taking less vacation then the industry average. Why? Because they have created a high-performance culture where employees hold each other accountable for producing results.

Nucor, the best-run steel company in the world, has mastered the art of creating a culture where employees hold each other accountable for performance. They achieved this by grouping their production-level workers in teams and then rewarding the team each quarter for its performance. The story is often told of a new hire who was added to a production team but was not carrying his weight. Did management have to identify and address the issue? Nope! His team members ended up chasing him off the site with large wrenches in hand. Now that's a performance-driven culture.

The following three steps are essential to building a high-performance organization.

Step 1: Performance metrics. Build within your system the metrics to measure performance. To do so you must first understand what success factors drive your business. Is it project profitability? Then measure revenue factor per project, which is utilization times direct labor multiplier. Is client satisfaction the key? Then get client feedback on employee performance. If schedule is the driver, track adherence to deadlines. If quality, track RFI's and change orders. The point is you need to have metrics to do so.

> *You must first understand what success factors drive your business.*

Also, make sure employees are measured on factors which they can control. For instance, revenue factor is highly dependent on great project management. So, a project designer may have little ability to influence its outcome, whereas it is a primary measure of the project manager himself.

Step 2: Regularly reward performance. As mentioned in Chapter 1, Millennials want instant gratification. While this is not possible in terms of profit sharing, waiting until the end of the year to pass out rewards is probably too long for them to make the connection. I have seen a number of firms, however, move to quarterly bonuses tied directly to key performance indicators. Some of these firm's stories are summarized in Chapter 9. This method is achieving great results and appears to be regular enough for everyone to make the connection.

Step 3: Stop rewarding poor performance: This may sound like common sense but it is not common practice in our industry. Design firm leaders often sacrifice driving firm performance in the name of peace, trying to avoid disgruntled average to poor performers. It is a losing philosophy. While there may be short-term gain in terms of not having to deal with difficult issues there will be long-term pain.

This is a critical issue for high-performance people of any generation and especially Millennials. Nothing is as demotivating as to be required to carry the extra weight of a poor performer only to see them rewarded the same as you.

> *Design firm leaders often sacrifice driving firm performance in the name of peace, trying to avoid disgruntled average to poor performers. It is a losing philosophy.*

In addition, you're not giving your poor to average performers the message they need to step it up. Oh, sure, you may yell at them and threaten but they eventually become numb to this as your words don't match your actions. While traveling the country training design firm principals, one of my favorite stories to tell is related to this topic. My wife and I have four wonderful

Case Study
Ensuring a legacy
Why performance-driven cultures promote firm legacy

In the early 1980s, Harwood K. Smith, who had built his Dallas design firm HKS from its first commission, found himself faced with seven young partners who wanted him to sell them control of his company. There had been little transition planning; the partners just felt it was their time.

As would anyone in such a spot, Smith had his doubts. He was being asked to give up more than 40 years of being in charge. But, after reconsidering, he realized he would have to let go of either the reins or his business. He wisely chose the former tack, and the future of HKS was ensured.

Smith's decision set a precedent for the firm's future generations. It signaled respect for the up-and-comers and demonstrated the importance of transition. And, in its wake, it revealed the importance of transition planning, which the firm has built into its culture.

Second verse, not the same as the first

The next generation came of age about 15 years later, in the late 1990s. At this point, Ralph Hawkins, current president and CEO of HKS, was serving on the firm's executive committee. A group of young principals came to him wanting to know when it would be their turn to play a stronger role in the firm. Smarter from experience, Hawkins knew that this time he needed a strategy.

"I had heard we would need 10 years to plan for transition," Hawkins says. "But we didn't have that much time, since some of the executive committee members then would be close to retiring. But I didn't want the leadership to go through the same thing Harwood did."

Hawkins figured the remaining tenure of each executive committee member and came up with a seven-year transition. He went to the executive committee and proposed a plan, which they accepted.

Bringing home a piece of the pie

Recently, the firm has asked its principals to return their shares at age 65, making it easier to bring their best and brightest staff in as shareholders— and harder for an outsider to take over.

"Not everyone passing 65 was interested in selling their stock," Hawkins recalls. "Some were concerned it would be like a demotion and that they would lose both power and financial security."

So the transition strategy focused on the very culture of his firm, which takes an unusual approach: they tie compensation to performance and to the amount of business an employee brings to the firm— rather than to the amount of stock an employee owns. At HKS, what's important is not how much you're worth, but how much you can contribute to the firm's earnings.

The outgoing HKS principals had no reason to worry. "This was all about keeping it internal, and it was all friendly," says Hawkins. "We assured them that their stock and compensation were never tied together, that they would remain principals, and that we would use their stock to ensure the firm's legacy."

It was an offer they couldn't refuse.

Baking more pie

After 63 years and two successful transitions, HKS— originally a one-man shop— now has offices in seven U.S. cities as well as two in the U.K., a staff of 525, and a gross income of $150 million. They have diversified widely — into health care, commercial, aviation, justice, sports, hospitality, education, and more.

Hawkins attributes HKS' growth to Smith's philosophy of bringing entrepreneurs up through the ranks and grooming them to lead the firm. In conjunction with this policy, HKS keeps its stock at a low value so that its most promising up-and-comers (encouraged by management) can continually buy stock; but they can't depend on it for retirement.

Says Hawkins, "Harwood Smith compensated people based on productivity— he never gave much emphasis to stock. A lot of firm owners boost their stock prices so that, when they retire, they will get the higher value. This makes it more difficult for younger people to buy stock." By nurturing its talent and making stock more affordable to the best, HKS ensures its own legacy.

children but, as you might imagine, four keeps you busy. To add to the challenge, our youngest, Stephen, is a special needs child. Learning basic tasks, such as speaking and anything requiring fine motor skills, is very difficult for him.

As such, potty training with Stephen was a monumental task. When he turned five, however, we started to make some progress. I effectively used my motivational style to encourage him by offering a trip to the ice cream store if he would poop in the potty. After some initial success, he started to lose interest. At the appropriate time of day, I would ask him if he wanted to go to the potty and he would look at me coyly and say no. I would offer ice cream if he went and he again would say no. Not long after he would have an accident. However, on our next visit to the ice cream store, he would get ice cream with the rest of them.

One day while teaching design firm principals not to reward poor performance, I had an epiphany. When I got home that weekend, I asked Stephen if he wanted to go to the potty. Same answer. I offered ice cream. Same answer and, very soon, the same results. So later that evening, I loaded up the car and took all four kids to get ice cream. I was smart enough not to bring my kind-hearted wife along. Once at the store, I started from oldest to youngest asking what kind of ice cream they wanted. The first wanted "cotton candy," next was "bubble gum," and then the third wanted some other weird flavor. (Whatever happened to chocolate and vanilla?)

When I finally got to Stephen, he was already excitedly pointing to his favorite flavor. I got down on his level, looked into his eyes and said, "Stephen, I would love to get you ice cream but did you poop in the potty?" His jaw dropped in despair. "Next time, I said, if you poop in the potty, I can get you ice cream."

> *Stop rewarding people when they don't meet the goals you have laid out for them.*

Now, here's the test. What do you think is the first thing Stephen wanted to do when we got home? You got it. He headed straight for the potty and sat there for an hour until he made a contribution. In fact, it clicked at that moment and he has been potty-trained ever since.

Recently, I was telling this story at a conference in Las Vegas when I caught a tear coming out of the eye of a lady on the front row. I stopped and told her that I really did love my child. "I know," she said, as the tears broke loose, "but I'm like your wife, you would not have wanted to bring me along either."

It is not easy to deal with poor performers, especially for us tenderhearted architects and engineers. We want to bring everyone along, but sometimes it can't be done. Stop rewarding people when they don't meet the goals you have laid out for them. It will give them the motivation they need to get there, if they can, and will more importantly energize your stars to stretch even further.

Not rewarding poor performance is as motivating to your star performers, if not more motivating, than rewarding excellent performance. Early on, I hired an engineer from the Boomer generation who was not able to keep up with the team and produce. I remember after our Christmas lunch one year, he came into my office thinking there must have been some kind of mistake. It's Christmas and he had not received his 'Christmas' bonus. "We don't give 'Christmas' bonuses on our team," I responded. "Only profit-sharing bonuses, and you did not contribute to our profitability this year. 'Christmas' bonuses promote a sense of entitlement. 'Profit sharing' bonuses communicate the right message. I'm not 'giving' you anything. I'm just allowing you to share in the success you helped deliver to the team."

SEVEN POINTS REVIEWED

Now that we understand the importance of first building a high-performance organization, let's focus on the message and meaning of each of Ryan Healy's seven points.

Points 1 and 2: What time do they have to be in the office? This is a great place to start. Millennials prefer a very flexible work schedule and design firm managers are reluctant to provide it. I know an engineering firm division manager who refuses to relent on this issue because he demands complete, face-to-face access with his employees whenever he wants it. For him, it is a matter of personal convenience. Perhaps if the balance of power was still with the employer his philosophy would work. But it isn't and it doesn't.

Case Study: Big Brother is Watching Your Firm!

What are the secrets to creating your next generation of leaders? Take some advice from the people who represent every firm's future. Inside Arch (*www.insidearch.org*) is an unusual, and scary, web site that posts opinions on design firms from those in an exceptional position to observe the real inner workings of a firm— past and present employees.

If this is the first you have heard of it, try the link! You put in your zip code and a summary of firm culture for all of the architectural firms in your area is provided for free. You may preach one culture, but this web site will let potential employees know how well you are 'practicing what you preach.'

At the top of Inside Arch's list of highest-scoring firms to work for is BauerLatoza Studio, a 12-person architecture and landscape firm in Chicago. Senior Principal Joanne Bauer believes there are four crucial areas of focus that contribute to readying her firm's next generation of top talent.

Joanne Bauer of the architecture firm BauerLatoza explains her firm's approach to hiring and developing a top-notch leadership team.

These crucial areas require the firm's principals to:

1. Be creative. When BauerLatoza Studio opened its doors in 1990, Joanne Bauer and her partner Bill Latoza gave a lot of thought to the business of running a business. "As architects, we want to be creative, and we tend to think of business as a necessary evil," Bauer said. She turned to her sister, an MBA, for help in setting up shop. "She helped me see that business can be creative," said Bauer, whose past experiences in large corporations taught her exactly what she didn't want to do in her own business.

Fifteen years later, the principals' commitment to a creative and supportive business structure is evident in the firm's internal growth development program, which focuses on employees' professional and personal growth. Features include:

- Frequent firm-wide meetings with business advisors, who discuss the growth aims of the firm as well as each staff member.
- Goal-setting for individual growth. Staff members work with a mentor to achieve those goals.
- Regular project presentations by every member of the staff. "The purpose is twofold: to teach everyone in the company about all other current projects so they're aware of what's going on, and to encourage everyone to hone their presentation skills," said Bauer.
- In-house computer skills tutors.
- Gym memberships and the use of a company-paid trainer.

BauerLatoza Studio's innovative development program earned the firm particularly high marks on Inside Arch. According to one reviewer, "It's nice to be treated like a human!"

2. Hire strategically. About five years ago, Bauer and Latoza began planning their firm's ownership transition. "We started very early, working with staff that expressed interest," said Bauer. And that meant all interested staff— not just senior-level employees. "Some of the best staff came in as entry-level," Bauer said. "We don't think of anyone as being too young."

Bauer looks for the strengths in each employee and is focused on building a well-rounded leadership team with a combination of talents rather than expecting one person to wear all hats. "Leadership skills are really hard to find," she said. "The goal is to find a combination of people with different strengths. A visionary, a rainmaker, and a good manager are all essential to the firm's leadership. We put so much into developing a team, so it's important to hire well."

3. Communicate constantly. All the creative planning and strategic hiring in the world won't succeed in building a great leadership team without one key element: communication. The partners provide individual and team reviews twice a year to ensure that expectations for success are clear, and employees are encouraged to discuss their ideas with principals. "The biggest investment for the principals is time," said Bauer. She and Latoza worked with leadership consultants who helped the partners reevaluate their own time management. "We saw we needed to stop managing so many projects and make time for this development."

Communication is essential when it comes to convincing potential leaders to take the leap into ownership as well. "One of the biggest challenges we face is to convince people to take that risk," said Bauer. "We have to communicate that ownership is exciting and not all fearful and scary— that it has more positives than negatives."

4. Think "team." Bauer recognizes that her firm's investment in its employees' development has huge payoff potential when it comes to ownership transition. "Whether we transition internally or whether it's external, it's very valuable to have this devoted staff," she said. When it comes to transitioning leadership, it is critical to support the team dynamic, which means taking a back seat to next generation leaders. "Allowing people to transition into the decision-making process is our challenge," Bauer said. "I have to concentrate on letting go and allowing things to be handled differently than I would handle them."

BauerLatoza Studio's commitment to staff development is showing positive returns, according to Bauer. "Our staff tells us we really are a studio— it's not just a name. People really do work as a team. It's about mutual respect."

I am, however, an advocate of core hours. We are in a business of collaboration where face time is important. Millennials actually prefer to work on teams and understand the need for collaboration to run a successful design firm. Yet I have found that you can achieve both by having 'core hours,' which are times when you are required to be in the office so collaboration can easily happen.

Some firms define these as 9 a.m. to 4 p.m., others as 10 a.m. to 3 p.m. The right mix is up to you, but allowing flexibility will increase productivity. How? By allowing people to come to work when they are most productive. For some mysterious reason, God created some of us to be morning people and some night people. I'm a morning person, normally doing my most productive work before lunch. Sometime in the late afternoon, my brain hurts. What I have found is I am most productive coming in early and heading home between 4:30 and 5 each afternoon. As a side benefit, it also helps avoid traffic congestion. After dinner and some time with the family in the evening, I'm good for some more focused time to work on whatever may need addressing.

> **For some mysterious reason, God created some of us to be morning people and some night people.**

Some of my team members come in earlier than I do, but some come wandering in closer to 9 each morning. As I have watched the latter group over the years, I've noticed they do some of their best work in the late afternoon and early evening. Now why would we want our team members in the office when they are least productive? Having core hours allows you to create a more attractive and productive work environment.

Healy also makes an excellent point regarding the 24/7 nature of our business today. I have some clients that, when they need something, call me about 7 in the evening on my cell phone. They do so because they know they'll be able to get in touch with me and it's often the first time of the day they can focus without being interrupted. That's business today. I want my team members to also be sensitive to clients' needs 24/7 and not just from 8 to 5. If that is the goal, there must also be flexibility in the schedule.

Again, these benefits will only work in an organization of high performers. If you have dead weight, they will take advantage of you. Although these bad apples will also clearly identify themselves for who they are when they do which will give you the opportunity to deal with them.

> *"I just had a Millennial employee leave my company and, during the exit interview, she explained several of these seven points to me. I thought she was crazy. Now I think maybe it wasn't her that was crazy. This will go a long way in building our team "the new way" as opposed to the old-fashioned way."*
> *— Responder from Minnesota to a blog on Millennials.*

Point 3: What's on his computer screen? A number of years ago, my firm began tracking "internet usage." The idea was to determine which employees may be abusing the system by spending most of their day surfing the net instead of doing their work.

After a few months on the program, I received a report from management that my three-star project managers all had recorded extremely high internet time. This came to me as a shock! These three were my top producers and biggest hope for the future of our organization. Perhaps the internet tracking system was a great management tool, I thought, because it is giving me information I did not have. Perhaps, as a good manager, I had an opportunity to provide constructive criticism in their lives to help them grow. So I sat down with all three of them in my office and explained how showing up on this report, even though I was confident they were not abusing the system, would not help them get where they wanted to go with their careers.

I count that as one of the biggest leadership mistakes I have ever made. Jim Collins, in his book *Good To Great*, says that if you have high performers on your team, the biggest challenge you have is not how to motivate them but making sure things don't happen that de-motivate them. I had made a critical miscalculation which soon became apparent. Turns out the high level of Internet usage showed up on the report purely because of a program called *WeatherBug* they had each downloaded. The program shows the current outside air temperature on the corner of your monitor. Unfortunately, to do so, it updates every minute, which our system recorded as a website 'hit.'

Less than an hour later, I received a scathing, and much deserved, e-mail response from one of them who had just determined the source. He also explained in detail how *de-motivating* it was to find out the company was more focused on petty 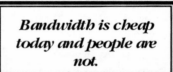 issues than performance. After realizing what had happened, I quickly apologized to all three, but the damage was done. It took some time and quite a bit of effort to get that out of their minds and it is never completely erased from memory.

Now, I understand there can be issues with bandwidth and having multiple people using the Internet can slow down the speed of the entire office network, but bandwidth is cheap today and people are not. Why make it an issue?

Also, as some Millennial responders to Mr. Healy's blog pointed out, not everyone can get their work done with these distractions present. I would agree. Again, it comes down to performance. If someone is highly productive, don't worry about their personal Internet usage, especially since these same people who may order something off of Craigslist during office hours are just as likely to respond to a client e-mail or do project work on their home computer after hours.

Another thing I've noticed about Millennials is they love to listen to music, usually in some type of MP3 format, on headphones while working. I even have one who has taken this to a new level. He has wireless headphones so he can get up from his desk to access the copier or printer without having to take them off. Now the previously mentioned division manager that wants people in the office when he's in the office also insists that his people do not wear headphones in the office. Why? Again it's related to convenience. He does not want to have to walk up to someone's desk with a question and wait for them to take their headphones off. I admit that I do at times find this frustrating. However, if a little occasional inconvenience on my part allows them to enjoy their work environment more, I'm OK with it. In fact, I believe the headphones also allow them to drown out the noise around them and focus more on their work.

To be honest, I would have loved when I was their age to be able to listen to music via headphones in the office. When I was spending all of my day behind a desk, this would have certainly been relaxing and enjoyable.

Point 4: His ultimately meaningless fashion statement. We reviewed in Chapter 2 how far our dress code has changed since we entered the business. As Healy mentioned, Millennials want to take it a few notches farther. Flip Flops and Crocs are their favorite footwear choice. In addition, I have found the Millennials I work with often have an aversion to shaving on a daily basis, just as Healy discussed in his article. While I'm not advocating relaxing the dress code completely in the workplace (I've actually had to let a few Millennials know their footwear selection was not appropriate), a relaxed dress code is

> *A relaxed dress code is essential in creating the right environment to attract Millennials.*

essential in creating the right environment to attract Millennials.

As professionals, we have been correctly taught we have an image to maintain and part of that image is certainly related to how one dresses and grooms themselves. I once read a book on consulting that advised when going to a client meeting, always dress equal to or at least one level better than the client. There's some truth to that, and we must teach our

Millennials to dress properly for client interaction, but while in the office, a relaxed dress code is preferred. Yet there must be limits because we are professionals, i.e. NO CROCS!!!

However, we need to determine and communicate those limits to our people.

Case Study
Circle of Excellence firm Jonathan Barnes Architects:
A low Turnover Culture

Jonathan Barnes Architects is a 9-person residential and commercial architecture, historic preservation, interior design, and retail, furniture, product, and graphic design firm in Columbus, Ohio. The firm's business manager, Chuck Redifer, shares the following about their culture.

Riding the development wave

Barnes was ideally positioned to become a principal player when the downtown Columbus, Ohio residential development boom began a few years ago. Around 75 percent of the firms projects are from repeat clients. "Mr. Barnes and our project people have great relationships with our key clients. We are oftentimes able to avoid the RFP process all together," explains Chuck Redifer.

The firm is looking to broaden its geographic reach beyond central Ohio by cultivating relationships with sub-consultants working on Barnes' current projects and getting them to introduce the firm to developers in other areas.

The prime differentiator

In cases where Barnes is in competition with other firms for the project, what sets them apart? The first differentiator is the quality of the design which according to Chuck Redifer, "sells itself." The second differentiator is Barnes' unique relationship with local building authorities and the firm's well-known expertise in interpreting local building codes. The firm's specific expertise with the code as it relates to older, historic buildings is highly valued by the clients of their downtown loft projects.

The firm is continuously working to build and expand their role as an authority on their core clients' businesses. Barnes is very active in the AIA and will soon assist in opening a satellite office of the Urban Land Institute in Columbus.

Maintaining focus in a small firm

There are times when the firm is working on 12 projects at a time and for nine people, that can be a tall order. How does the firm keep people motivated and focused? "It's the little things," says Chuck Redifer, "taking a half day one day and having weekly firm-sponsored lunches reminds people that we are all in this together – working to achieve the goals of the clients and the projects." Turnover in a firm this size is a significant threat. To mitigate this threat, the firm is also careful to take care of every person individually, starting with providing competitive salaries and bonuses.

Early this year the firm also introduced a traveling fellowship program. "Twice each year we will send an employee to a city of his or her choice for an extended weekend to see what other firms around the world are doing architecturally. Upon returning the employee presents the trip to everyone in the office over lunch."

The Plan Going Forward

Chuck Redifer is certainly optimistic. "We work with really smart people. We look forward to extending our reach far beyond Columbus on the strength of our people."

Point 5: Anything he does at happy hour. Here's another point that requires balance. Healy makes a great point that the focus should be on performance at work versus other issues, and we all know personally that the college years, as well as those immediately after college, are not the times we always make our best decisions.

Yet we have a responsibility to teach them professionalism. They need to understand their actions out of the office inevitably affect their performance in the office. Inappropriate relations with a co-worker can create tension in the workplace. I believe there lays an opportunity here for mentors to share lessons learned and help Millennials to 'grow up' in this area.

Point 6: His "lack" of experience. Ah, now this certainly brings back memories. As I read Healy's sixth point, some of the faces of the 'old' people in my first design firm (heck, they were ancient, must have been at least in their late 40s or early 50s) popped into my head, scolding me about my poor lettering and drafting skills and complaining about my lack of real-world experience. "Kids these days," they moaned to each other.

I remember over lunch in the break-room one day finding out how old one of the particularly grumpy ones was and exclaimed in amazement, "Wow, you're as old as my father!" Note to self, this was not an effective way to "Win friends and influence people."

And today the refrain continues. They grew up in a different world than we did. We understand how we learned values such as work ethic, honesty, and integrity in the world we grew up in, but we don't understand how they could have learned those same values in their world. Second verse, same as the first.

There is another challenge in our business we face related to this point, however, in regards to their confidence, or overconfidence, mentioned in Chapter 1. In areas where experience matters, which are abundant in our field of practice, we must apply our experience to their work. The difficulty is figuring out how to do so without killing their motivation.

A few months ago, one of our Millennials who reports to one of my Gen Xers, came into my office frustrated that they were being 'micro-managed' by their boss. "He reviewed and questioned a bunch of issues on my project's design," they said. I abhor micro-managing. Yet, when I got the other side of the story (and there is always another side) the manager expressed concern that his Millennial was working beyond their experience level and resistant to input. "How," he asked, "can I keep from squelching their motivation without compromising the quality of the work our firm produces and exposing us to avoidable risks?" Great question!

I believe the answer lies in understanding design quality. First, there are issues related to one's design that our experience will show may result in unnecessary change orders, increased bid prices due to risks, and system failures. These issues are easy to identify as such and must be addressed. However, there is a second type of design issue that is much harder to discern and

> *Solutions, especially in architectural design, are rarely based on right or wrong, but rather good versus better versus best.*

that is related to 'opinion.' Solutions, especially in architectural design, are rarely based on right or wrong, but rather good versus better versus best, and these answers often differ based on the tastes and styles of the person making them. Even in the engineering field, many decisions also fall under this classification.

To answer my Gen X manager's very astute question, he must first learn to differentiate between the two issues. When a design falls into the first category, he must require it to be addressed and explain why experience has shown it is an issue. When an issue falls into the second, he has to use more judgment. He may share his opinion as to how he would do it differently but always allow the designer to make the final choice. This will empower them, as well as show them the wisdom of experience if they choose their own direction only to discover later that it really was only good, instead of best.

Now, again, you may want to toss this book out the window. This is your firm! Your name is on the sign on the building! It's YOUR style that must be reflected in every design. While I agree there are standards, even styles, a firm must maintain and it is important the end product coming out the door on various projects looks like it came from the same company, if you micro-manage every design decision, you will choke the creative life out of your best Millennials. The loyal followers, who lack creative drive, may stay, but the superstars that could one day continue your legacy well into the future will do so for someone else or for themselves.

Point 7: His personal calls. As before, the message here speaks again to the importance of creating a performance-driven culture. If I have someone whom I know is going to be there when the job has to be completed no matter what time it is or what day of the week it is, should I care if they make a personal call or two in the afternoon?

Now, if he's in my office going over one of his projects with me, then I do expect him to ignore the call and return it later, but I have never experienced this to be a problem.

WORK/LIFE BALANCE

Millennials want to do more than let their careers consume their lives. This is a difficult idea for a lot of today's design firm principals to swallow. Traditionally, you come out of college and sacrifice your life for a firm in hopes of achieving partnership someday. In the past, this model has worked fairly well as our business has been about selling hours and there have been no shortages of workaholics. The unspoken

> **Our business has been about selling hours and there have been no shortages of workaholics.**

rule was you sacrifice for the existing partners by subordinating everything else in your life to your job and someday you'll receive the benefits of becoming a partner. Today, this model has lost its appeal. Millennials do not want to spend their careers putting family, and other interest on hold until retirement.

Recently, a cousin of mine graduated with a Master's degree in accounting. She went to work for one of the largest accounting firms in the country and began to kill herself in pursuit of partnership. Eighty-hour weeks all on the road were commonplace, and I was told by others I knew in this firm that my cousin was definitely on the partner track.

After five years of this ridiculous pace, the partners offered my cousin a partnership in the firm. She immediately turned in her resignation.

Perplexed, I inquired as to why she put in all that effort if she did not plan to accept partnership once it was offered. Wasn't that her goal in the first place? Actually, I found out, it was. Remember, Millennials are achievers and she achieved her goal. However, she realized the life of a partner, although financially rewarding, was going to require her to continue to subjugate everything else to that cause. This was not what she wanted.

The great news is that if you have the right people in your firm, and have a well-thought-out strategy that you execute religiously, you can produce financial returns for yourself and your employees that are well in excess of the 15-20% average returns our industry produces, AND you can do it without killing yourself or your people! As mentioned in the introduction of this book, I have had the pleasure of being a part of a team that has consistently been producing returns more than twice industry average and yet have been able to maintain a reasonable pace for myself and the team's members.

How? I'm often asked that question. Normally, design firm principals are looking for one answer. "What's the ONE thing I must do to be a top performing firm?" Well, problem is, there's not one big thing. This question reminds me of an encounter a sports reporter had years ago with the Vince Lombardi, the legendary coach who led the Green Bay Packers to wins in the first two Super Bowls.

"Coach," said the reporter, "your teams win an awful lot." "Well, that's true," responded Lombardi casually. "Yet," continued the reporter, "I've noticed that your team really doesn't have the best athletes of any team in the league," continued the reporter. Lombardi agreed. "I've also noticed that they are not the biggest or even the fastest players in the league," the reporter continued. "So how is it you manage to win so

> *The team that blocks and tackles the best usually wins the game.*

much?" Without thinking for long, the coach responded, "When I first started coaching football, I became a student of the game. After a while, I began to notice that more times than not, the team that blocks and tackles the best usually wins the game. So when training camp begins each year, we start by working on the fundamentals of blocking and tackling."

In response to the question "What's the ONE thing we need to do to be a top performing design firm?" I usually share this story. It's not one big thing that puts you over the top, it's doing all the little things right on a continual basis.

The most fundamental of those little things is, in the words of Jim Collins, author of *Good to Great,* "Getting the right people on the bus." In other words, to become a top-performing firm in any business, the very first step is to get great quality individuals on your team. It's interesting the circular benefit created here. If you get the right people, as a whole, you will not have to work as hard to generate superior results. As a consequence, if you don't have to kill yourselves to create superior results, you will have created an environment that will attract the right people, which in this case are the type of Millennials who can deliver excellent results within a reasonable timeframe.

One place to start is by demonstrating a good work/life balance yourself. I often feel that I may be setting the wrong tone when I'm not the last one in the office every day. Yet one of our young Millennials, when asked what it is he likes about working with us, said, "I like it that your wife calls you at the office and you always take the call." After discussing it further, I realized the message he wanted to communicate was I, and the other senior team leaders, demonstrated a desire to maintain our own work/life balance. Because we were 'practicing what we preached,' he believed he could also achieve this balance in his life while being a member of our team.

FIRM CULTURE

Healy's list is not complete. There are other firm cultural traits that also attract high performance young professionals.

Open communication. Millennials want to know how they are doing and how the firm is doing. They want to be in the loop, if you will, on decision-making in the office. For instance, on our team we like to have interviewees talk to everyone in the office either formally or informally and then get input from everyone on the hiring decision. This allows us to let everyone be involved in the process, increases the chance of "buy-in" with our team, and often gives us a unique perspective on potential candidates.

One consistent theme from the PSMJ *2008 Circle of Excellence Conference*, a panel discussion of CEOs from A/E firms ranked in the top 20% in terms of performance, was

"…people want financial transparency." Nowhere is this more true than with Millennials. I'm often asked to what level and breadth should this information be disseminated and how. In general, Millennials do not need an annual balance sheet or income statement. They wouldn't know what it meant if they had one. What they do want, however, is a realistic understanding of how the company is doing, and more specifically how their compensation is tied to their personal, team, and firm success.

After four months behind a drafting table at my first engineering job, I noticed the workload slowed down, yet no one wanted to talk about it. After six months, I was laid off with half the people in the office. Last one hired, first to go. Interestingly enough, layoff day was my birthday. I'll never forget sitting in the front conference room early

> **People want financial transparency.**

that morning eating birthday cake the receptionist had brought in with the rest of the staff when the branch manager walked in the front door, realized what was going on and let a disappointed look briefly pass across his face. He was the only one in the entire office who knew what the day had in store.

I constantly tell my team I'll let them know how we are doing as a team and a firm so there will be no surprises. I can't promise in our cyclical industry that the picture will always be rosy, but you won't get blindsided like I did my first year out of college. This allows your team members to relax and focus on their work instead of worrying about their paycheck.

> *"Although they are better educated, more technologically savvy, and quicker to adapt than those who have come before them, they refuse to blindly conform to traditional standards and time-honored institutions. Instead, they boldly ask, 'Why?'"*
> – Eric Chester from *Employing Generation Why.*

Sense of purpose. Millennials are very concerned about the environment they live in and their impact on that environment. Not only in terms of 'saving the planet,' but they are concerned about helping others. More than a job, the best ones are looking for a career where they can make a difference.

This is a huge opportunity for A/E firms to sell the vision and goals of the practice relative to sustainable design, energy efficiency improvements, building affordable housing, improving education or research through the built environment, etc. Most firms have some internal goals that, when achieved, 'make the world a better place.' By making them a core part of your firm's culture, communicating them to current and potential team members, and celebrating every success made in achieving them along the way, you can create a magnet for talented Millennials.

> *Most firms have some internal goals that, when achieved, 'make the world a better place.'*

Don't be a "Cake Eater." While you should always take your work seriously, the office environment should be fun! This is probably the most important point relative to culture. We have had multiple recent graduates turn down competing offers from our competitors for slightly more money. When asked why they chose to accept ours, they always say the other office's culture seemed stuffy and uptight. Ours, however, gave them the sense we focused on achieving and delivering excellence in everything we do while still having a good time and always keeping an eye on work/life balance.

Is Burnout Driving Away Your Staff?

Are you the type of person who "gives my all," no matter what your doing. That's an expectation that most of us have of our employees, too. If we're leading our teams well, we've motivated employees to want to do their best and work hard for the firm.

Unfortunately, it's easy for employees to cross the line into burnout in the name of "hard work" and dedication.

One way to make sure your team members aren't being overworked is by calculating utilization rates— the amount of billable time charged to projects. It might seem counter-intuitive that an extremely high utilization rate is bad, but it's almost a guaranteed indicator of unbearable stress on your employees and will ultimately damage your firm.

All too often, we see firms over-utilizing just about every staff member. Why? Because they can't hire enough people to perform the work they've taken on. The more "chargeable" (or "utilized") your personnel, the less time is available to them for training, marketing, and instituting process improvements— the very glue of your organization.

To calculate the utilization rate of your project managers, divide the direct project labor for PMs by the gross payroll for PMs. If this number is higher than 75 percent, you've exceeded the optimal utilization rate. The over-utilized PM is neglecting client relations and marketing, and rapidly losing her or his educational edge. Maximizing the efficiency of your staff is an admirable goal, but not if it compromises their ability to perform.

At PSMJ Resources, we've found that the ideal utilization rate for technical staff is 90 percent. Because technical staff do not interact as frequently with clients, their utilization rate can be higher than that of project managers. Your firm-wide utilization rate should be no higher than 65 percent.

In a conversation about this with PSMJ's research director, Bill Fanning, who has long studied the issue of utilization rates and their impact on firm performance, Bill shared this insight: "Now is a great time to examine your projects and clients, find out where you're not making money, and then say 'No' to losing propositions. Principals really need to take a critical look at their firm's operations and use people more effectively on work that is profitable."

I recently asked five of the Millennials on our team why they chose us as a career choice instead of the other companies from which they had offers. Without hesitating, one young civil engineer said, "Because you guys are not 'Cake Eaters'." I had to write that one down. "What in the world is a 'Cake Eater'?" I asked while recognizing the other four Millennials present knew exactly what he was talking about. He told me the phrase came from the movie "The Mighty Ducks" and describes a person or organization that is too stuffy. Wow, nice to know I'm not a "Cake Eater," and in the future I'm going to stick with pie.

For the past 10 years, our team has held an annual Disc Golf Tournament (a Millennial sport) complete with prizes and plaques. We have Friday afternoon picnics once a month in the summer at the picnic area in our office park. Afterwards, we sometimes go to the Go Kart track to burn a little rubber. In the winter, there's Paintball, and in the summer, we have the office annual movie premiere night where we all go on opening day to the agreed-upon movie. By the way, one of our superstar Millennials leads this program. He's a movie connoisseur and picks our annual movie premiere as much as six months in advance, makes the arrangements, purchases the tickets, and builds excitement in the office as the date approaches.

Around the office are pictures and trophies from the events, helping visiting Millennials quickly sense this is a fun place to work. We decided to add movie posters from the annual movie premieres we have attended. Why? It is a great way to communicate some of what we are about to potential new hires. When touring the office they ask the question themselves. They certainly don't see movie posters in other offices. It is a great way to start the conversation about our culture.

Making Volunteerism a Firm-wide Goal

Millennials want to give back to their communities and be a part of something bigger than themselves. Are you interested in getting your firm more involved in the community, but not sure how and where to start? Use the following seven steps as a model for building a voluntary service program, as provided by author David C. Forward, author of *Heroes After Hours: Extraordinary Acts of Employee Volunteerism*.

1. Identify your purpose. Be honest. Why use the company's financial and personnel resources to promote employee volunteerism? Is it to enhance the corporate image, to stimulate employee morale, to address problems in the community that disturb you? There are no right or wrong answers here. But if you don't identify your motivation for creating this program, you are asking for trouble later on.

2. Determine employee interest. Depending on whether you plan to launch the program in a limited way, such as with one department or geographic location on a trial basis, or with all departments starting the volunteer program simultaneously, you need to sample employee interest first.

3. Establish the structure of your volunteer effort. Who is going to set up this new program? An outside consultant? You? Once established, will it fall under the aegis of human resources? Community affairs? Public relations? Or are you small enough for it to report directly to you? The Points of Light Foundation (*www.pointsoflight.org*) research shows that department managers responsible for employee volunteerism initiatives spend on average 20 percent of their time managing the program. Do you have an extra 20 percent of each day you could give to help the project grow?

4. Define your corporate commitment. The two "M's" here are management and money. Studies of employee volunteer groups nationwide indicate an extremely strong link between employee morale and the participation in service projects by top management. Will your company include corporate and employee volunteerism as a goal in its mission statement? Has senior management approved the budget and made the financial commitment to support the company's volunteer program?

5. Determine your community's needs. Talk to your local volunteer center. They are rich sources of information on community needs. If there is no such agency in your town, try the Chamber of Commerce; the Rotary, Jaycees, or Lions Clubs; the Boy or Girl Scouts; or leaders of the places of worship. Do not forget two excellent sources of information for community needs: the local newspaper and your employees.

6. Establish employee volunteer recognition activities. Employees rarely list "recognition" as one of the reasons why they volunteer. Yet a photograph in the staff newsletter showing them volunteering can be a source of pride.

7. Decide how to evaluate success. The most common way to evaluate the success of a volunteer service project is to ask participants to complete a survey form. At the end of the year, you can compare that year with the overall objectives set at the start of the program. If you don't have the time to do this, delegate this important task to an employee or community service consultant.

Technology. Don't skimp on technology. To do so will ward off the most talented Millennials. They grew up in a world of high-speed networking and understand the language better than we do. With the pace in which technology changes, this is a particularly difficult challenge.

Recently, I sat in a division manager's meeting where a disagreement occurred over whether the company should provide desktop phones for college interns and young graduates. In reality, the argument itself is behind the times. No one in this age group comes into our offices without their own cell phone with e-mail and texting capabilities.

Providing laptops, PDAs, and cutting-edge software are essential differentiators that can help set your firm apart. The good news is this generation has the ability to get the most use out of these tools and drive the productivity of your firm.

Leadership Behaviors that Build Strong Firm Cultures

What is it that makes one office sizzle with positive energy, excitement, and innovation? What makes another tired, frustrated, and uninspired? The culture. And how do firms build a culture of success? It starts at the top.

Do your principals visibly support the firm's values, purpose, and success— to the extent that your whole staff "walks their walk?"

Do your employees follow the principals' lead in committing to outstanding customer service? And through modeling your firm leaders, do your employees believe in each other enough to work out differences within the team?

Here are six leadership qualities to help you realize these ideals.

Strong inspiring leaders:

1. Embrace and develop intelligence throughout the generations. Many firm leaders allow a gap to develop between themselves and the up-and-coming generation. To keep ideas fresh and innovation alive, there should be partners in each of the following age groups: 35-45, 45-55 and 55-65. Successful firm principals constantly build their next generation of leaders.

2. Envision what they want and make the changes needed to get there. In successful firms, owners lead, not manage. They engage their staff in a greater purpose. They envision where they want to go, fill their staff with the thrill of that vision, and make whatever changes are needed to get there. Finally, the entire firm is able to shift its behavior in the intended direction. Vision is dynamic; it changes and grows over time.

3. Hire the best and brightest staff. To create a dynamic, evolving, and attractive work place, good leaders hire only the best and brightest people. Fortunately, this is not difficult; employees seek these employers because their reputations precede them— their firms are thriving. The best and brightest employees are achievers who feed on innovation and creativity.

4. Work as hard as everyone else, or harder, because they are excited about what they are creating. Owners who want remarkable work places are excited about their potential, and work side-by-side with their employees—guiding and encouraging, sleeves rolled high.

5. Take on the tough issues. Leaders do not shy away from conflict or tough issues. They are open to challenge and coaching. They are alert to what they hear and see. They use a filter of experience and maturity to make sure they are informed of what may not be readily apparent. They are particularly sensitive to gaps between their talk and their walk. Great leaders don't avoid, but rather take on, the challenges that are key to their success.

6. Have a sense of humor. Intelligence and humor are strong companions. When work is fun, people laugh at themselves and don't take themselves too seriously. You grow and adapt faster to your environment when you can learn from mistakes.

CHAPTER 4

Leading Millennials

"A 60-something graduate recently reflected: 'We wanted what they want. We just felt we couldn't ask.' Herein lies the truth: What young workers want isn't so different from what everyone else wants. However, young workers are asking for it."

– Karen Cates and Kimia Rahimi,
"Mastering People Management,"
Financial Times, November 19, 2001

In the previous chapter, we reviewed design firm cultural traits that attract Millennials. How about the relationship with their boss? How important is that to today's young architects and engineers? Figure 4-1 shows data from a study of factors that motivate engineers done by management theorist Frederick Herzberg. Although the data from this particular study came from engineers, I have found it also very much applies to architects, interior designers, land surveyors, and the other types of professionals that make up our industry. The results of his study really challenge some of our traditional thinking on motivating employees.

First and foremost, salary is not as big a motivator as we often think. Out of nine factors studied, salary finished in the middle. In fact, salary can be as equally de-motivating as motivating. Now, don't think the message is you don't have to pay your people well. You must! However, after reaching acceptable rates, relative to the market you are in, you are not going to achieve long-term motivational results by increasing salary. Don't believe me? Try this test. Think about the last time you received a raise that was more than you expected. Was it motivating? Of course it was, but for how long? What I mean is how long did it take before the same issues that frustrated you in the organization were again frustrating you at the same level? I have asked this question to design firm principals across North America and I always get the same answer: One, maybe two weeks at most. Now, is that a great return on your financial investment in motivating the troops?

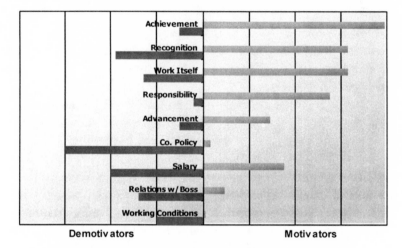

Figure 4-1: Herzberg's Motivational Factors (For Engineers)

The top four motivators are a sense of achievement, recognition, the work itself, and the amount of responsibility one is given. My research into Millennials revealed these four issues are more highly valued by this age group than any previous generation.

My favorite leadership teacher, Dr. John Maxwell, wrote an excellent book entitled *25 Ways to Win With People*. One of the particular ways Dr. Maxwell outlined that really rang true for me was giving personal, hand-written notes to your people recognizing their achievements and expressing your appreciation for the value they bring to your team and the firm. I have found this to be a powerful way to convey both appreciation and recognition and, as a consequence, instill motivation. Out of the many bosses and supervisors I have had in my career, only one ever took the time to write me a note of appreciation for my efforts. I still have that note to this day. How much does it cost? Maybe 50 cents for the card. How strong is the motivational potential? I can tell you from personal experience it is much longer than two weeks!

I travel frequently by plane. So, to hold myself accountable for writing notes, I always keep a few in my carry-on bag. My goal is on every trip to write at least one note. The time on a plane just before take-off or landing when your computer has to be off anyway is a great opportunity. Try it for yourself and watch the results. Giving Millennials, or any employees, regular, well-thought-through feedback is a key to building a high-performance organization.

This was recently reinforced to me at a leadership conference where Jack Welch, the recently retired CEO of General Electric, was asked this question. "Mr. Welch, as CEO of General Electric, the largest company in the world, what one activity did you spend the largest percentage of your time on?" Great question! Without even thinking twice about it, Welch replied, "I spend 70% of my time…." At this point in the sentence, I was already amazed. How could the leader of the largest organization in the world spend 70% of his time on any one activity? I was confident he would say 'strategic planning.' I was wrong. Welch continued, "I spent 70% of my time on employee performance evaluations." I was in shock. Welch went on to say he was personally responsible for reviewing 500 employees four times a year and was involved in the review of many others as well. And to think we can't even find the time to properly give employees feedback once a year.

> *My goal is on every trip to write at least one note.*

Isn't it peculiar the biggest de-motivating factor, with almost no potential to motivate people, is company policy? There's a very good reason for this and it is certainly applicable to Millennials. To understand how it works, first think of *why* companies need two-inch-thick employee manuals? Now, I'm not talking about the couple pages you

Mostly Business by Ted Go

"I don't have time to write performance reviews, so I'll just criticize you in public from time to time."

need in there for legal reasons, but the rest of the material explaining in great minutiae the details of company rules and regulations. Is it to manage your star performers? Not at all! You need it to manage your dead weight, the people being dragged along by the organization who are always looking for a way to take more than they give. For instance, do you think the architectural firm that has no set number of days off has to devote five pages of its employee manual to vacation policy?

In recent years, updates to Herzberg's study have revealed the category 'relationship with the boss' has now become the biggest potentially de-motivating factor in the workplace. In a similar finding, data taken from the 2007 PSMJ *A/E Bonus & Benefits Survey* revealed the number one reason people list for leaving a firm is "Personal Reasons." What does that mean? More times than not it means my boss is a jerk and I'm not going to tell you. Poor relationships with the boss are the number-one reason people leave firms.

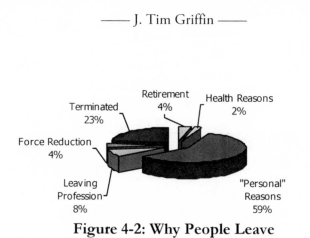

Figure 4-2: Why People Leave

So, there's good news and bad news. As the boss, if we have a difficult time keeping Millennials, we are most likely the biggest part of the problem. That's the bad news. Good news is we also are in the best position to be part of the solution. On this issue, we, as the manager, control our destiny. There's no one else to blame. I don't know about you, but I wouldn't want it any other way.

MILLENIAL MYTHS

"...the majority of Millennials are still kids. And, despite the facts, they're getting a bad rap. You're familiar with the handbasket theory. It's as old as time. It says, 'Kids just ain't no good these days.' It says, 'Today's kids are going to hell in a handbasket.'"
– Claire Raines in *Connecting Generations: The Sourcebook*

The first place to start in improving our ability to manage Millennials is to dispel some of the myths upon which we may wrongly base our approach with them. If our methods are based on false assumptions, they are bound to fail.

Myth #1: Kids today are hopeless. You may be surprised to find that in the last two decades serious crime among teenagers has declined dramatically, teen pregnancy is falling at the fastest rate ever recorded, and serious drug use among teenagers has dropped. In addition, today's teens are less likely than previous generations to abuse alcohol or drink and drive. Yes, there are some bad ones out there, but overall this is a more 'responsible' generation than their predecessors.

Advice for Millennials – Strive to be a Seller-Doer

A recruiter for our industry recently wrote the following recently in the *Professional Service Management Journal*:

I hear it all the time from my clients: "We need a seller-doer. We need a seller-doer." Not only is it a tight market for technically strong and competent civil engineers, it is even more difficult to find my other favorite classification of engineer, "The Rainmaker." So now clients ask us to uncover the perfect combination: not only someone who can make the rain, but someone who can analyze it, purify it, bottle it and get it out to the customer. This is the power of the elusive seller-doer.

It is imperative to learn and understand the pure design and technical requirements of your profession — whether you are focusing on designing tunnels for transit authorities, laying out 7,000-acre master planned communities, or preparing architectural plans for an esteemed university. Learn the technology, learn the concepts, study up on the corresponding codes and ordinances and prepare yourself to receive your professional registration as soon as possible.

However, do not fall in the trap that many young architects and engineers so often do by getting stuck behind the computer in their cubicle all day. Get out! Be proactive in learning the client and business and marketing side of things at an early stage in your career. You can accomplish this by practicing the following tactics:

* Ask your manager if you can tag along on some client meetings from time-to-time.
* Request to attend community planning meetings.
* Sit in on presentations, contribute to the preparation of proposals, and attend the occasional industry conference.
* Make presentations or write papers for conferences.
* Attend specific marketing and business development workshops.
* Of course, you need to balance your deadlines and technical training with your education in the art of client care and business development, just don't get bogged down in only the nuts-and-bolts for your first seven or eight years.

Don't sit on the sidelines and wait for those opportunities to come to you — go find them — and find them early on in your career. This way, by the time you've got 10 years under your belt, you will be able to pass out business cards with your name and the title of "Seller-Doer."

"In the real world, young people behave better than any generation in decades."
– Mike Males, "Ignore Fear Mongers; the Kids are Okay,"
San Jose Mercury News, April 29, 2002

Myth #2: Millennials are Gen X Squared. Often people assume Millennials are no more that Generation X on steroids. In other words, they have the same strengths and weaknesses as their predecessors, but somehow they are worse. This is definitely not the case. In fact, Millennials are very different than the generation that preceded them. A lot of the excesses of Generation X drove Millennials in the opposite direction. As an example, Gen Xers like to work independently while Millennials prefer to work with teams.

Since members of these two generations are very different, using the same management style with each is not likely to be successful.

"…The Millennial Generation will entirely recast the image of youth from downbeat and alienated to upbeat and engaged – with potentially seismic consequences for America."
– Neil Howe and William Strauss, *Millennials Rising*

Myth #3: They are not at all like Boomers. Boomers, who are two generations removed from Millennials, often look at the new arrivals to the workforce with bewilderment. As a consequence, often the assumption is made these two generations have little in common. Actually, the opposite is true which should be expected.

Generations tend to swing as a pendulum toward the opposite extreme of the previous generation. For example, Generation X's primary motivation was money. Millennials, on the other hand, tend to value a number of other things as well, such as life balance, being sustainable, and giving back. If history repeats itself, which it does, the generation to follow Millennials will most likely be similar to Generation X.

As you read about the environment in which Millennials grew up, you see some similarities to that of the Boomers' formative years. For instance, Boomers were also raised in 'child-centered' homes. In fact, not only was the home that way, the entire society was forced to revolve around this generation based on its significant size. Also, just as Millennials have a desire to 'give back,' Boomers rallied to President Kennedy's cry "Ask not what your country can do for you but what you can do for your country." Theirs was the 'Peace Corps" generation. Just as Millennials want their voice to be heard, Boomers were very vocal in response to the Vietnam War and other politically charged issues.

Myth #4: Millennials' desires are different from ours. No matter what generation you grew up in, are Millennials' desires for the workforce that much different from what you and I would have liked? Who would not have preferred a more relaxed dress code? I know I sure hated having to wear a tie to work every day on my first job. For one, the three ties I had (all with paisleys) were not going to be enough to get me through the week.

How about a more flexible work schedule, a desire to work on 'important' work, and a good work/life balance? Are not these all things we would have liked to have? In reality, a lot of their desires for the workplace were ours as well. So what's the difference? Because of the shift of power described in Chapter 2 from the employer to the employee, Millennials have the ability to ask and get some of these things where previous generations did not.

MILLENIALS AT WORK

As with any generation, Millennials have both strengths and weaknesses that help and hurt them in the workplace. Understanding them can help you get the most benefit from their strengths and help them, and you, overcome their weaknesses. Let's begin with strengths:

Strength #1: Positive Attitude. Millennials are a can-do generation. They have been told all their lives they can do anything they put their mind to. What a shot of adrenaline this can be in our firms. Harness this energy! Give them challenges and Millennials will attack them with a vengeance.

Strength #2: Goal Oriented. Millennials are used to having numerous goals and achieving them. They are not, however, used to setting the goals. Normally parents, teachers, or coaches set the goals for them. So, give them goals on a regular basis and clearly outline what is expected. Also, ask them regularly to set their own goals. On my team, I ask every member at the beginning of each year to list their goals for the year with a due date no later than the end of January. The goals should include personal training goals as well. Then, at the end of the year and during annual reviews, we monitor how they are doing. As a side note, I set personal goals on the same schedule and share my goals with the team. They hold me accountable.

Strength #3: Multitasking. All their life they have had to juggle multiple tasks and priorities. Significant demands from high-performance schools, as well as sports, music, etc., drew them in numerous directions. As a consequence, they do not have to focus on only one task at a time. They don't even want to. So, load them up and let them manage multiple tasks. They have a gift for doing this. One of our Millennials

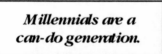

Millennials are a can-do generation.

who had been with us for a year turned in their input forms for the upcoming annual review. More than once this employee noted how they thrived on multi-tasking and preferred this to being bored. Boredom is one area I have always found can easily be addressed in our business. Load them up!

Strength #4: Team Orientation. Millennials prefer working on teams to being a lone ranger. This is great for an industry such as ours where collaboration drives both quality and creativity. So put them on teams! Encourage team collaboration and reward teams for succeeding together. Millennials have been preparing all of their lives to excel in team environments. Set up your office spaces in ways that encourage collaboration and idea sharing.

Strength #5: Technical Savvy. If ever there was an area most members of previous generations need help, using technology to its fullest potential is one. Also, as our industry continues to move more into relying on technology to manage and produce our services, these skills are becoming more essential. Use your Millennials to help you understand and fully utilize the benefits of technology.

Companies such as Siemens have set up reverse mentoring programs, where Millennials actually mentor older generations on technical issues. Jack Welch said that "e-business knowledge is usually inversely proportional to age and rank." He's right. Use this strength to your advantage.

Weakness #1: Overconfidence. Confidence seems a funny place to start in listing weaknesses. The positive attitude side of confidence is certainly a strength but when it crosses the line to overconfidence, it is a dangerous weakness. Millennials often desire to take on tasks beyond their experience level and do not appreciate being reigned in.

> *Set up reverse mentoring programs, where Millennials actually mentor older generations on technical issues.*

My advice is to give them a little more than enough rope to hang themselves and provide a safety net for when they do.

This is one of the most difficult aspects of managing Millennials. It's about balance and it is a difficult balance to find. Work to help them understand you want to add the value of your experience to their talent and enthusiasm. Over time, they will grow to trust you more and their experience will begin to catch up with their confidence. We'll discuss how to turn this weakness into a strength in Chapter Eight.

Weakness #2: Impatience. Millennials are not used to waiting. They get bored very quickly. In addition, they have never experienced a real downturn in our business and thus have no real appreciation for what the ugly side of our cyclical business can feel like. To be honest, I hope they never find out.

As a consequence, however, they get frustrated quickly when things do not happen as fast as they think they should. Mix overconfidence with impatience and you have a dangerous combination.

I had a Millennial on our team who came on as a co-op, joined us after graduation and got his Professional Engineering License. His nickname was 'the Machine' and what a producer he was. Even as a co-op student, he was obviously a rare talent. Combining this high level of natural talent with his Millennial confidence, he was the true definition of a 'superstar.'

I believe you should always put your best people on your biggest opportunities and not on your biggest problems. As such, I moved this young man into a new area of business which I thought had tremendous opportunity. In reality, however, I underestimated the potential opportunity and it quickly became even more than I had

> *Always put your best people on your biggest opportunities and not on your biggest problems.*

imagined. Having a superstar working on this opportunity was a Godsend. However, I quickly realized it would grow beyond what he could himself handle based on his limited experience, even though he was operating well beyond his years.

Creating an Atmosphere for Teamwork

1. Create team spaces. Every project needs a center, a "locker room" where the team can get together and find out the status of things. Without a separate space for the project effort, you'll have a fragmented team, with members operating in different areas of the office. This situation can inhibit team building. It can hurt your scheduling, budgeting, and project performance.

So pull your teams together. Give each project its own "team water cooler"— a physical space, or at least a central bulletin board. In this space, PMs can post a project "to-do" list, as well as schedules and assignments. For Millennials, who thrive in virtual worlds, the 'physical space' can be virtual via a project web site. Team members can put up messages. Creating this team center will help build a sense of camaraderie and keep everyone dancing to the same beat.

2. Communicate! Get people together at least once a week to talk about what's going on with their project. If a team has had no meeting for a month or more, you're asking for trouble. If it has had no meeting during its entire course, you're asking for disaster! Team building takes communication. And communication takes the effort of the project manager to bring team members together at regular meetings to share what's on their minds.

3. Clarify your purpose. The project "cause" comes out of the project manager's expectations for the job. Team members must know those expectations. Make sure your PMs share their objectives with team members at least once a week— the regular team meeting is the perfect time. Otherwise, don't be surprised by poor project performance. When it comes to motivation, PMs may not have much more to do than create an environment supporting self-motivation. Your aim is to have your teams understand the project "cause" and rally 'round what the PM is trying to accomplish.

4. Create a collaborative work environment Provide an open office environment that encourages team collaboration. Low cubicle walls, naturally lit open areas, and offices without doors all help. A human resource director recently told me open office doors promote collaboration while closed office doors promote destructive rumors.

So, I brought in a very talented Generation X manager to help take the lead in this area and manage what has turned out to be a rapidly growing team in a very dynamic market. Later, however, I found out the original Millennial was frustrated he had lost the opportunity to fully lead this growing team. He felt like I had pulled someone else in and put them in a place where he wanted to grow. After discussing it with him, I can certainly see how he could have felt that way. In my eyes I was protecting this young engineer from taking on more responsibility than his experience could possibly handle, thus risking frustration and burnout, while also recognizing his vast potential for growth in his career over time was limitless. Plus, the size of the opportunity provided more than enough room to grow for them both.

The key is communication, and to be honest, initially I handled this poorly. It was not until after the changes were made and he eventually shared his frustrations with me that I was able to more effectively communicate. I guess the reasoning for what was done seemed obvious to me. Now, however, in light of what I have learned from Millennials, I can definitely understand why the wrong message was originally communicated to him.

> **Good leadership is required to properly implement change.**

Understanding how Millennials think and view the world has helped me, and will help you, recognize how an impending change will be viewed by your Millennials before it occurs. Seeing the change through the same lens Millennials use will help you to present and frame it properly. Ultimately, this is what real leaders do. Effective management is essential in our firms, but it involves only the day to day operational activities. Good leadership is required to properly implement change. Therefore, knowing how your Millennials think helps you be a better leader.

Myth #3: Inability to deal with difficult people.
Because of the cocoon of protection in which Millennials
grew up, they often have little experience in dealing with
difficult people. This can cause problems in many areas. For
one, some of the talented professionals in our firms are
sometimes rough around the edges. Even if this is not the
case, we all have clients that can be difficult and
unappreciative. If that's not enough, there are code reviewers
for government agencies and municipalities to boot. In other
words, there is no shortage of difficult people in our line of
work.

I have especially noticed a challenge with some of our
Millennials in dealing with difficult clients. There is almost an
amazement among them that people who think illogically and
react emotionally exist. Herein lies a great opportunity for us
to help them grow. For one, Dale Carnegie's book *How to
Win Friends and Influence People* is an excellent training resource.
A number of years ago, we took all of the people on our team
through that book over several lunchtime seminars. This
investment has paid huge dividends!

Weakness #4: Distaste for menial work.
Millennials want to feel their efforts are making a difference
for the organization. This is hard for them to do when they
are running around making copies and coffee for others.
Traditionally, however, we use our least experienced people
to do the menial tasks. Certainly makes sense from an
efficiency standpoint. So, how do we overcome this barrier?

First, try to send as many 'menial' tasks as you can to
administrative assistants and others who are not architects
and engineers in training. Second, when giving a task to a
Millennial, take the time to explain how it fits into the big
picture and why it is important to the organization. Third, get
over the attitude that you had to do it when you were their
age so why shouldn't they? Remember, times have changed.

Make People Want to Work for You

At a recent PSMJ Resources *Project Management Bootcamp*, PMs chose these characteristics as the most important when a leader is building a devoted team:
* Have a good track record
* Be a good mentor and teacher
* Be dedicated to the team
* Help with making decisions
* Value team member contributions
* Listen
* Be organized
* Share credit, but also shoulder the blame (in public)
* Offer candid feedback (in private)
* Keep a positive attitude
* See and create opportunities for the team
* Actively solicit input
* Challenge individuals
* Maintain an environment that is not volatile
* Let the team know what is expected at the project's outset
* Be clear with project objectives
* Delegate effectively

In her book *Connecting Generations: The Sourcebook*, Claire Raines writes that Millennials want to be challenged, treated respectfully, learn new knowledge and skills, work in friendly environments, have flexible schedules, work with positive people, and be paid well. Employers typically go wrong when they don't meet Millennials' high expectations, discount their ideas for lack of experience, allow negativity, or feel threatened by their technical knowhow. That's certainly a challenging list for even the best manager. However, by embracing as many of these 'wants' as possible, you can attract, retain, and empower the best high performance Millennials.

As a leader of Millennials, I have found if you can use this knowledge to create the right environment in which they can thrive, they will blow your socks off! Their energy will be contagious and your team's impact and results will be phenomenal.

Happy Employees Speak Volumes About Your Firm

Smart employers are investing more in their firm's first and greatest asset— their employees. To find out how they can keep their people happy, insightful firm owners are not only uncovering the needs of their staff members, but addressing them.

Without question, your staff has strong and valid opinions about the desirability of your firm as a workplace. If you don't know what these are, it's time to ask!

"What makes our company a great place to work?" is all you have to say. The answers will reflect your firm's values and culture. A successful firm is a place where people thrive, so define what it is about your workplace that employees value most and build upon those features!

The following five HR basics provide methods for uncovering employee needs and guarding your greatest asset.

1. Complete employee performance reviews. It's good practice to meet informally with all your employees several times a year for performance reviews. Meet with new employees three times or more in the first year.

Ask your employee to make a list of his or her strengths and weaknesses; let him or her do the talking! Next, affirm the employee's strengths, and add any that may have been missed.

Then discuss your straightforward concerns about weaknesses. The ratio of strengths to concerns should be 3:1. And a good rule of thumb is to limit your concerns to two or three of the most important ones.

End the review by asking your employee to write a growth plan and return it to you within a week. The plan should be about a page in length with two to three bulleted items stating areas of weakness and how they will be addressed. It should also include requests for training, on-the-job experience, coaching, and mentoring.

Don't ask for this information unless you are willing to provide what is requested. Advise the employee to retain a copy, and file the personal development plan in the employees' personnel file.

Also, whenever you do employee reviews, do them on time! This is so simple but rarely occurs. Why? "Well, I meant to do the review on such and such a date but that unexpected project issue, fire that had to be put out, etc." is what I hear. It's all nonsense! When you do a review late, you are communicating to your employee that they are not important, at least compared to these other issues.

With technology available like Microsoft *Outlook*, you can send yourself reminders two to three weeks in advance. Schedule your reviews at least a week early, to allow time for the inevitable unexpected event. Just do it. Failing to do a review on time is a stupid way to de-motivate your team.

2. Link specific performance criteria to increased compensation. Your employees must be compensated equitably in the marketplace. Develop a plan to address any shortcomings. You need to remain competitive in your industry if you wish to retain your people. (For a copy of PSMJ's latest *A/E Management Salary Survey*, call 800-537-PSMJ.)

3. Start a program for advancement of key personnel. Implement a training and development plan that will build the management and leadership skills of key employees, supervisors, and managers. Your team leaders and project managers have the most day-to-day contact with your employees, so train them in the skills they need to help everyone succeed.

You can retain key personnel by communicating the criteria for success, and fast-tracking promotions for those who meet the mark. Identify what you want to reward— leadership, supervisory skills, sales, recruiting, project management, coaching— and create a plan to financially compensate the successful development of these skills.

4. Establish diversity training programs. Get team leaders off the production mode and into a true leadership mode at least 25 percent of the time.

Employees will look first to their immediate supervisor for support and communication, but only if they are available to provide it. Train all supervisors to:
   * Be effective in employee performance reviews
   * Develop their own professional growth plan
   * Support their staff in generating their development plans
   * Communicate training opportunities to all employees
   * Communicate potential career paths to employees

5. Improve communication and establish trust. People stay in environments where trust and communication exist. Employees want to trust your firm, their supervisor, their team and its ability to produce a great product. If you haven't already, develop two-way communication systems. And respond in an honest, straightforward manner to your employees at all times.

Ask employees regularly: "How are you doing? Is there anything that you need?" Following through on their requests increases their loyalty to your operation.

CHAPTER 5

Recruiting Millennials

"They combine the teamwork ethic of the Boomers with the can-do attitude of the veterans and the technological savvy of the Xers. At first glance, and even at second glance, (Millennials) may be the ideal workforce-and ideal citizens."
> – Ron Zemke, Claire Raines, and Bob Filipczak,
> *Generations at Work.*

I grew up on Tobacco Road, in the heart of the Atlantic Coast Conference, one of college basketball's premier conferences. Within a 20-minute drive from my home are three members of the ACC, each of which has won multiple NCAA tournaments titles over the years. In this highly competitive environment, there is little tolerance for a coach that cannot quickly build and maintain a winning program. As such, it has been an interesting study in leadership to analyze the styles and traits that makes successful coaches' teams consistent winners over the long haul.

FIRST THINGS FIRST

Over the past 50 years, the game has changed dramatically. The physical height and size of players has dramatically increased, even while the speed of the game has accelerated. Instead of traditional 'student athletes,' the NCAA has become a training ground for lucrative careers in the NBA. Where four years of college ball was once a given, some star athletes bypass college altogether and jump right into the NBA draft. Many of the top selections from the 2008 draft were underclassmen.

As the game has changed, the success or failure of a program has become more and more dependent on RECRUITING!!! While training programs and game-day strategy are still important, X's and O's have taken a back seat to the recruiting process. The coach that can consistently win with mediocre talent comes along at the same frequency Miami, Florida sees snowstorms.

Today, most strategy discussions focus on recruiting the best talent. *Sports Illustrated*, as well as many other media outlets, tracks and rates the relative success by college or university of each season's recruiting class and, consistently, the teams that rate highly in this contest, start and finish seasons with high rankings.

WHAT CAN WE LEARN?

So, what tips can we translate from the world of college basketball relative to recruiting talent in our industry. Here are some suggestions:

Focus on recruiting. College basketball coaches have five or six assistant coaches, and their priority throughout the season is recruiting. The coaching staff meets at least weekly to discuss recruiting strategies and review potential prospects. Assistant coaches keep the roads hot visiting tournaments and building relationships with high school coaches. It is not one of the things they do, but it is the most important thing they do.

The first thing we can do is involve all of our firms' key leaders in developing our HR strategy, as well as personally leading the charge in identifying and recruiting potential candidates. Just as one assistant coach, in our case our human resources manager, may take the lead, everyone is involved. In addition, the head coach (CEO) is also actively involved and always available to do whatever is necessary to help close the deal with a promising recruit. Make it a firm priority!

So how do you encourage your key leaders to focus on recruiting? Well, assistant coaches know their success on the recruiting path leads directly to their future success in college basketball. Great recruiters are highly valued in any program. Is that true in your firm?

Sell the culture. Great coaches know they are competing with many other programs for the best talent. To win, they focus on selling their culture. From the moment a potential recruit arrives on campus, they are met by a host who leads them through a detailed and well-thought-out schedule. They see the facilities, walk past the trophy case, and are inundated with the program's history, as well as plans for the future. They also tour the campus to get a feel for what being a student there is like.

Do the same with your candidates. Focus on selling your culture. What is your firm about that would appeal to them? Do you stress a great work/family life balance? Is it a fun work environment? Or is it a driven, high-performance organization that rewards its stars? What is it about your firm that will set you apart from your competitors?

On my team, we emphasize that we are a high performance team but we also have fun and don't take ourselves too seriously. Since our competitors have a tendency to come across as 'stuffy,' this really sells, especially with the younger generation.

Use their peers. When a potential recruit arrives on campus, they are greeted by a host who will stay with them throughout their visit. This person is usually a peer. Who best to sell the college's benefits than another student? They also will spend time with other players…same idea.

Use your young people in recruiting. In my firm, when we are selling a recruit, we have them spend time with some of their peers…especially the ones who have been other places and value the benefits of our organization. This is a powerful differentiator, and sets the candidate at ease.

IT'S A NEW GENERATION

In the early 1970's, the great John Wooden, who coached UCLA to 10 national titles, a feat likely never to be repeated, had a star center on his team named Bill Walton. Wooden had strict rules for his team members concerning dress code and appearance. Even though the Flower Child generation was now well entrenched in our nation's universities, Wooden required a strict military-style haircut.

For opening practice one year, Walton, wanting to make a statement concerning his coach's antiquated ways, showed up to the first practice with hair that had not seen scissors in months. Early in the practice, Coach Wooden walked up to Walton and inquired about his plans for getting his hair cut. When Walton stated he had no plans, Wooden calmly looked and him and said, "Well, Bill, we're gonna miss you." Walton showed up at practice the next morning with his locks shorn.

I love a good story like that, but often hear similar sentiments expressed by today's firm leaders relative to the Millennial generation now entering the workforce. "Why should I change for them? No one changed for me when I started in this business! They should have to conform to us!"

Nice sentiment, but there is a serious flaw with this reasoning. Wooden had the most successful program in the history of the NCAA and correctly assumed Walton needed him more than he needed Walton. When today's firm leaders entered the workforce, we were entering an employer-leveraged industry, where the employer had all of the power. This has changed. You rarely see a quality candidate at any level of experience that does not have multiple offers from competing firms. So unless you too have a program as successful as Wooden's (hint, most likely, you don't), you are going to have to focus on creating a culture and leadership style that Millennials find attractive.

I have watched once great coaches fade quickly in recent years because they could not adapt their styles to the new generation. They held firm that it was their way, or the highway, not realizing that the proverbial road they were referring to would eventually be for them. In contrast, some coaches have made adjustments to their leadership styles and morphed their programs to match the ever-changing generational needs. As a result, they continue to win.

Remember, it's not about you......it's about winning!

DON'T LOWER YOUR STANDARDS

With the ever-increasing trend of high school and college basketball players jumping early to the NBA, coaches have had to adjust their recruiting strategies. When the trend first started about 15 years ago, many coaches tried to focus on finding good talent, instead of great. The idea was finding good players who did not have the ability to jump too early to the NBA would build team continuity and lead to success. It didn't work.

Today, the best coaches have accepted and embraced the trend, realizing that having stars on the team was critical to winning; even if it was unlikely they would stay beyond their freshman year.

Often, I have seen firm principals fret over the difficulty of keeping their stars happy and home. It's not an illusion. Star performers are needier than average performers, and your competition will hear how good they are through shared clients or other avenues. However, to build a high-performing organization, you must have high-performing people. Don't focus on the fear of losing them. Instead, do everything you can reasonably do to keep them around for the long term.

WHAT'S IN IT FOR THEM?

To adjust to the growing attractiveness of the NBA, great coaches now sell themselves to potential recruits as a career resource. For instance, coaches often boast about the number of players from their program now playing in the NBA. And when Draft Day approaches, they help their players analyze and understand their prospects, explaining the risk/reward potential of the decision to jump early. What I have found is the best coaches focus purely on what is in the best interest of the player, instead of their program.

Why not focus on talking them into staying? Because it would be chasing short-term rewards at the expense of the long term. Future candidates are most interested in what the program can do for them and want a coach that will focus on their best interest.

A couple of years ago, I had a young engineer on my team, who had been a tremendous performer, walk into my office to say he had made a personal decision to go into the financial planning business. My heart sank! However, instead of trying to talk him out of his decision, I encouraged him, knowing that he would be successful with whatever career direction he chose. I did emphasize if it did not work out, he could always come back, but as best I could, I tried to focus on what was in his best interest.

I'm sure word spread. If your people ever were to get the impression that the business was more important to you than them personally, the damage will be great. Don't let it happen. Focus on being a resource to help all of your people reach their full career potential, even if that were to mean changing industries.

As a side note, a few weeks after completing the draft of this chapter, this same young man unexpectedly called me on my cell phone one day. After two years of pursuing financial planning, he had come to the conclusion that although this career path could be very rewarding from a financial perspective over the long haul, for him it was not as personally rewarding of a career path as being a professional consulting engineer. He wanted to come back! Wow, what a powerful addition he would be to our team. Plus, what a powerful message he can share with other Millennials concerning the advantages of our industry compared to others. He rejoined our team less than a week after he first called me.

I have seen coaches encourage their young players to test the draft market and confirm their potential market value without signing with an agent, which would prevent them from being able to return to college basketball. Often, these players do find it is in their best interest to stay longer in college and work to improve their future marketability. A smart coach is able to welcome them back with open arms. I am glad I did not burn any bridges with my young engineer in a foolish attempt to talk him out of what he already had his heart set on. Just as a coach, I have a returning player who is now able to fully focus on developing his career as an engineer and he's doing so on our team. Wow!!! I could not be more excited!

> *A smart coach is able to welcome them back with open arms.*

THINK LIKE A COACH

The race to attract the best and brightest to our firms is more intense than at any time in the history of our industry. It is also more important as well. With increasingly complicated designs, a less skilled contracting industry, growth in the use of information technology, and clients who are demanding tighter and tighter schedules, the need for excellent employees is, and will continue to be, the key differentiator between average and high performance organizations.

So, think like a coach....we have a lot in common.

THE BEST WAY TO ATTRACT
HIGH PERFORMANCE MILLENIALS

We've already addressed our problem: For the past 15 years, the number of A/E degrees awarded in the U.S. has been on a steady decline. And if that is not bad enough, fewer and fewer of this smaller pool of graduates are joining our business. The consequence? If you think it is hard to find talented Millennials now, you haven't seen anything yet.

However, there is a silver lining: if your firm can identify and attract a steady flow of Millennials from the shrinking pool without having to dramatically increase total benefit packages, you will increasingly gain an edge over your competitors. Easier said than done, right?

Developing talent through the "farm system". With this goal in mind, some leading-edge firms in markets that do not support high fee structures have attempted to model the farm systems of baseball programs by trying to identify potential talent early. Since very few firms can afford the New York Yankees' strategy of outbidding for proven talent, this is a reasonable approach, but most often the results are mixed.

Traditional recruiting consists of figuring out what kinds of people you need, advertising, and hiring them. Unfortunately, most firms need the same kinds of people: senior professionals and PMs. And we already know— they aren't available!

The solution is to turn your recruiting strategy upside down by:

* Recruiting the best Millennials you can find.
* Only recruiting Millennials who have the potential to eventually be project managers and senior level professionals.
* Putting them on the training fast track and keeping them for the long haul.

Tips from the best CEOs in the A/E Business

At a 2008 roundtable discussion of firm leaders representing firms performing in the top 20% of our industry for the previous year, the following quotes on recruiting and retaining were recorded:

* "You need to find passionate people. Quality and talent attracts quality and talent."
* "We insist that our design staff be on a licensing track. We have an intern development representative that helps young designers get licensed. This has been a great benefit to us in recruiting (Millennials)."
* "We sell prospective employees on the sexy projects and the niches we serve. We show people where they fit in the firm now and in the future."
* "We have a first-time home buyer's program for new staff."
* "Growth potential and stock ownership programs are attractive recruiting tools because everyone can buy stock."
* "You need to have a great place to work. Provide good benefits-then sell them on the firm."
* "We use training as a recruitment tool. We budget for staff training in our business plan and we let the candidates know."
* "Millennials need more continuous performance feedback than Baby Boomers and they want to be involved early in the critical path on projects with clients."
* "It is the obligation of (Millennials) to understand the boss and where she is coming from-not just the other way around."
* "We use a 40-item checklist to prepare as a firm for a new employee's arrival. We assign a new employee a mentor that guides them through the first week and beyond. We provide an indoctrination sheet-a checklist of items that we are sure the new employee knows about the firm and the environment very early in the process. We arrange for new employees to have lunch every day the first week with different departments. We facilitate frequent department "lunch and learns.""

* "Each employee has an IPDP, Individual Professional Development Plan, that provides an ongoing career track over a one- to five-year period. People leave firms when they do not get opportunities-and everyone realizes and seizes opportunities differently in our firm and the IPDP helps us prevent that from happening."

* "We believe that there are simple decisions that affect morale. Little things mean a lot. We give all employees a restaurant gift card on their birthday and we provide Friday breakfasts and we subsidize the soda machine because not everyone drinks the free coffee. If employees request new (or second monitors) or new office chairs, we get them. The costs of these items pales in comparison to the cost of losing an employee."

* "We do comprehensive performance evaluations— they are annual, formal, and we do not skip them. People need confirmation and feedback— so we also offer it informally on an ad hoc basis."

* "Do lots of little things right. Even small firms like mine can do little things that are big."

* "We have a ping pong table for employees to use to blow off steam. Periodically, we employ a massage therapist and use the ping pong room to provide our employees with stress-relieving massages."

* "There is clearly a shortage of up-and-coming architects. We are in the Minneapolis-St. Paul area and we offer a $1,000 renewable annual scholarship to an architecture student residing within 100 miles of our firm that maintains a 3.0 GPA. We do this to generate interest in having the student strongly consider coming to work with us upon graduation."

* "We make it a point to keep employees' spouses happy as well."

* "Over the last four years, our firm has gone from 600 to 2,400 employees. Growth can create unprecedented opportunities for staff and we have found that this has limited turnover."

* "We offer an adoption program for employees-a benefit not covered by regular maternity and family leave options."

* "Our culture provides an environment for individuals to help colleagues flourish. We make it a point to give younger employees more opportunities to grow. We have a robust training program."

This requires a long-term view of recruiting, but if you do it right, the rewards are well worth the wait. So where do you find the kinds of Millennials you can develop into your future stars? You probably won't find them at college job fairs— the best ones have already been picked up by other employers. Instead, you have to identify potential stars at least a year before graduation.

Here are some creative ways that design firms are doing this today:

* A surveying firm in the Southeast donates equipment to a local college with a strong surveying program. In return, the firm gets "first dibs" on the best graduates.
* An architectural firm in the Midwest offers zero-interest student loans to outstanding juniors. If the student comes to work for the firm, they forgive the loan at the rate of 20% per year, so that it is entirely forgiven if the student stays for five years.
* A national engineering firm offers a $1,000 prize to a student with the best Master's thesis, and $1,000 to the professor. For just $2,000, they get to see samples of work from top candidates in the top universities. And they get great PR in the bargain.
* One principal I've worked with at an international structural firm based in British Columbia moonlights as a professor in the structural engineering department of the local university. He's really a spy, however, using his night job to identify the best structural engineering students and bring them on board.
* An engineering firm in Louisiana identifies local high school seniors who have done very well at math and science and works with the school's counselors to direct those students to enroll in engineering.

Offering scholarships to smart high school students will certainly bring some candidates into the right degree programs and ultimately into your office, but there are no guarantees they will develop a passion for what you do, fit in with your individual company's culture, or possess the people and common sense skills necessary to develop into a productive principal. Good grades are not necessarily an indication of any of these traits. Ultimately, you're making a risky investment now and hoping for a return way down the road.

A Better Way. What if there was a strategy guaranteed to ensure every Millennial you hire out of college would be productive the very day they walk in the door; enhance your company's culture; increase your company's marketing reach; and help respond better to the cyclical nature of our workload, all for no upfront dollar investment?

Sound too good to be true? Perhaps, but I have personally seen all of these goals achieved through the effective implementation of a college co-op/intern program. This program, available at most engineering schools, as well as some architectural schools, encourages undergraduates to spend up to three semesters working full-time in an associated industry prior to graduation. Our division, within my current firm, began this program 10 years ago. Since its beginning, the majority of our college graduate hires have come through this program. In fact, our pool of good candidates from the program has exceeded our ability to grow. The results? We have had to pass on good candidates so we could focus on acquiring only the best. That's right! Even in a strong business climate, we have had to pass on good candidates so we could focus our effort on hiring only the best.

As I travel the country talking with various firm principals, I always get the same response to this story. "Hey Tim, next time you pass on a good candidate, can you send them our way?"

Don't have an engineering school near your office? It doesn't matter. Find it hard to compete with benefit packages of other industries? We have actually had multiple cases where our graduates turned down a better financial offer elsewhere so they could join our team. In fact, to date we have only had to one offer rejected. However, after a couple of months at another firm, this candidate changed her mind and came back to join us. Today, she is a high performing team member with a bright future who is quick to let others know how good they have it at our firm.

Picking the best. I mentioned our co-op program at a PSMJ *Principals Bootcamp* and it generated many questions from the audience. One of them being, "How do you screen potential co-ops?" One of the five qualifications I mentioned was that when trying to identify excellent candidates, we don't focus on how high of a GPA they may have. We don't ignore GPA, but we

> *Work ethic, personality, good common sense, people skills, and passion are a must.*

believe it to be a poor indicator of potential to develop into an excellent principal in our business. Work ethic, personality, good common sense, people skills, and passion are a must. Our success has been phenomenal.

One of our Millennial hires, however, did receive a 4.0 from a nationally recognized engineering school and finished as valedictorian of his class. He also turned out to be a superstar, but it was the work ethic, personality, good common sense, people skills, and passion that impressed us about him in the first place, and not the GPA.

As with any strategy, an effective co-op program has to be both well-planned and diligently executed or the results will be poor. So let's review how to develop an effective strategy, the screening process, the right environment for success, and the other benefits associated with using college co-op and internship programs to win the battle for great talent.

How to Pick the Best Talent in a College Co-op Program. To better understand student motivation, I completed a survey of a number of current and former co-op students to determine primary reasons for entering the co-op program. Answers included earning money to reduce school loans and a need for a break from school, but the two top answers were "I wanted to increase my odds of finding a good job upon graduation by adding experience to my resume" and "I wanted to know what engineers really do through hands-on experience."

These answers highlight that engineering, as an education choice, is somewhat unique in the professional service industry. Most architectural, medical, education, law and other students typically know what they want to do upon graduation and have a reasonable idea what the career may entail. Engineering students, however, often enter college unsure of which discipline they ultimately want to pursue. In fact, I have yet to find a potential co-op student that had their eyes set on the A/E industry when entering college.

Fertile ground. Herein lays the opportunity. By identifying the right candidates and creating the proper experience, future professionals can find a home in our industry and within our organizations. They also can find, develop and demonstrate a passion for what we do and begin a career path that will be both challenging and rewarding.
Here are four steps to begin collecting resumes from which you can identify the best candidates:

1. Get to know the co-op liaison on campus representing the discipline you are pursuing. These folks have quotas and are highly motivated to help you meet your recruiting goals. Let them know your needs. They can be your biggest advocate.

2. Get to know the professor who teaches the class most likely to have the right candidates. Ask if you can visit and make a pitch for your company at the beginning of class. This can generate a lot of resumes. Also, offer to speak at one of the student chapter meetings (such as ASHRAE, AIA or ASCE). These organizations tend to attract the more mature students.

3. Attend campus co-op job fairs. They usually occur once a semester.

4. Start early! This can't be overemphasized. If you are looking for fall candidates, start in the spring. We start looking for spring candidates in early September. If you wait until a few weeks beforehand, you only get the procrastinators and leftovers.

This may seem like a lot of effort, but once you have hired graduates from the program, you can begin to entrust them with the above tasks. They will be excited to have the opportunity, it will be great training, and they can better relate to the students. Plus, they will do a better job with these tasks than you can.

Finding the potential stars. The best starting point is to heed Covey's advice from his book *Seven Habits of Highly Effective People* and "Begin with the end in mind." As with any investment, it's the long-term rewards that are most valuable. When looking for talent through a co-op program, start by identifying who you want them to be in 10 years. Ask yourself, who are your most effective team members now? What are the traits driving their success and productivity? Here's a potential checklist:

> *"Begin with the end in mind."*

* Depth of technical skills
* Ability to be a team player
* People skills
* Work ethic
* Passion
* Big-picture thinker
* Communication skills
* Common sense
* A self-starter
* Great leadership skills

The list, and order of priorities, is completely dependent on your firm's vision for the future, the market you serve, and your focus for delivering value to that market. Know which skills are necessary for your market and target those skills.

> *There are no guarantees with any investment, but you can work to increase the odds of success.*

Next, ask yourself about the likelihood of candidates wanting to be long-term players. Remember, there are no guarantees with any investment, but you can work to increase the odds of success. Here are some questions to consider:

1. Are they likely to want to live in your locale after graduation? If a student is already from the area, the odds are greater.

2. What are their plans upon graduation? Do the students intend to begin a career or pursue an advanced degree? Don't be afraid to ask. One candidate actually told me he intended to start his own consulting firm as soon as possible, which was nice to know!

3. When do they anticipate completing their degree? Is this reasonable timing with future hiring needs?

Networking with Generation Next

The best tools for networking with Baby Boomers don't always translate with younger generations.

Moseying up to a barstool and talking shop with a potential client over a few drinks. Sharing the fairway at the country club with a couple of high-profile public-sector clients to pick their brains as to who they might recommend as viable candidate for an open VP slot in your firm. These always have been and always will be the best ways of networking at a high level with your Baby Boomer peers. As we all know, your Baby Boomer peers are retiring and people from a new generation are moving up.

My question is, how current are your networking skills to the Millennial generation? How can you equip your people to get in touch with this generation of students and junior engineering professionals who are internet savvy and using social networking web sites like MySpace (www.myspace.com) and Facebook (*www.facebook.com*)? After a few years out in the real world they transition into more professional oriented networks like LinkedIn (*www.linkedin.com*). If this is all a foreign language to you, hit the books (or at least the web sites) for Social Networking Web Sites 101.

Assuming that you have at least a vague understanding of what I am talking about, do you know that, on both MySpace and Facebook, you can find different groups like ASCE, and ASCE student sections? Did you know that schools like Syracuse University and Virginia Tech have their own MySpace pages specifically for their schools of architecture? A company web site is great, but you need to expand your exposure to the tech-savvy potential hires of today. It is easy to develop a MySpace or Facebook page that you can promote within the trade associations mentioned above, and many others as well. You can even start your own group (what a great way to generate loyalty and name recognition!). Post jobs, announce big project wins, discuss market conditions, highlight current projects and update it once a month. When your firm attends university career fairs, make sure you have a couple of laptops at your table where students can see that you are current and that you understand their generation, they will be impressed as you flash them your Facebook page.

LinkedIn is the professional version of MySpace and Facebook, and it is a natural transition for regular users of those sites. People love to see their accomplishments and bios on the internet. Explore different groups or start your own. According to Matt Barcus, the president of Precision Executive Search, Inc., a Pottstown, Pennsylvania-based executive search firm specializing in the civil engineering community, you can search for potential candidates by plugging in your competitors' names or keyword phrases like "civil engineering" or "environmental planner" and see the results.

Cultivate fertile ground. You can identify the best talent, but without the right environment they will become bored and disillusioned. During my own co-op experience with a multinational company, I spent an entire semester bored to tears trying to look busy. I did not return for a second semester, and even questioned if engineering was the right career choice for me.

Size was not the problem; smaller A/E firms are not immune. I have talked with numerous former co-ops that hated their experience and did not consider returning to these firms after graduation.

Ultimately, it is not your job to make co-ops succeed, but it is your job to create an environment where they will thrive. The following steps will help:

Step 1: Identify a mentor for each co-op. Hold this mentor accountable for establishing the proper environment.

Step 2: Lay out a plan for all three semesters with each student at the beginning. For example:

- *Semester One Goals:* Become proficient with CAD; begin involvement with field work.
- *Semester Two Goals:* Begin involvement in design related activities such as renderings, load calculations, model construction, and independent drawing of sections, etc.
- *Semester Three Goals:* Design and oversee construction on a small project from start to finish.

Step 3: Get feedback at the end of each semester to determine how you, and the mentor, are doing.

Step 4: Establish a payment plan upfront. Our firm has a rate at which we hire all first time co-ops, based on survey information from each school's co-op department. We then offer a $1/hour increase with each returning semester, and another dollar bump if they successfully pass an optional course offered by their school that focuses on the technical aspects of our business. It's more than worth it to us if they do because they return with additional skills.

Step 5: Offer interesting opportunities. Small projects provide something for the co-op student to tackle from beginning to end. Also, don't keep them in the office all the time. Get them out to the project site, to a client meeting, or to an interview.

It sounds easy, but it isn't. Inevitably, we tend to lose our focus in this business due to the onslaught of never-ending deliverable deadlines. The tyranny of the urgent too often usurps the important. Though, to be successful, you must constantly monitor the program's progress. If it was easy, anyone could do it. The fact that it is not easy is why a successfully designed and executed program creates a competitive advantage.

To summarize, when formulating your co-op/intern strategy, begin with end in mind, find the best potential candidates, and give them an environment in which they can grow. The rest is easy; you just watch the cream rise to the top.

FOUR CO-OP PROGRAM STRATEGY TIPS

Tip #1: Pass it down. Once you have established your program and have hired your first graduate from the program, pass primary responsibility for continuing the program on to this person. They can market for new candidates by attending co-op career fairs and speaking at on-campus opportunities in the classroom and through student trade organizations. They are in the best position to relate to a college audience and will value the opportunity.

Next, let this employee do the first round of interviews. The candidates will be more comfortable opening up, and it is a better use of resources.

How to Become a Talent Magnet

Jack Welch, former CEO of General Electric, and his wife Suzy, former editor of the *Harvard Business Review*, wrote an article entitled, "How to Be a Talent Magnet" (*Business Week*, September 11, 2006). In this article, they identified six "gold stars" needed to be a preferred employer. These points are presented below, along with our commentary as to how they relate to the A/E industry.

1. Preferred employers demonstrate a real commitment to continuous learning. Every A/E firm I have ever met says that its people are its most important asset. And we see the younger generation of employees demanding training the way they demand health insurance: as an essential employee benefit. But on average, A/E firms invest about a third as much per employee on training and development as the *Fortune* 500. If your firm can just be average compared to the *Fortune* 500, you will stand out from the pack of most of your competitors.

One firm that stands out is the 300-person engineering company FMSM. The company has hired a former professor from the University of Texas to teach in-house technical courses. These courses are part of "FMSM University," a continuous learning program that focuses on professional, technical, and leadership development.

2. Preferred employers are meritocracies. Salary surveys of our industry have consistently shown that the two most significant variables that determine compensation are (a) type of degree and (b) years of experience since obtaining that degree. Among managers, the biggest variable determining compensation is firm size. Is that how a meritocracy is supposed to work? I don't think so. But there are plenty of exceptions. An extreme case is a 60-person architectural firm in Texas that pays all its architects a base salary equal to one-half of the market rate, then makes it up in quarterly bonuses tied to firm and individual performance. This firm has been extraordinarily profitable and its architects have averaged twice the annual compensation of their peers in more traditional firms.

3. Preferred employers not only allow people to take risks but also celebrate those who do. And they don't shoot those who try but fail. Our industry's record here is a bit better, especially in the small and mid-size firms. But many large firms we know are highly risk-averse and punish anyone who takes a risk and fails.

One company who empowers employees is Goetting & Associates Consulting Engineers, a 75-person MEP engineering firm in San Antonio. The company places extra emphasis on finding employees with an entrepreneurial bent. One of the company's main goals is to find people who can think independently and generate new opportunities. Goetting & Associates also gives project teams full control of the project: they get work, write proposals, plan projects, produce the project, keep clients happy, do billing, and get paid for invoices.

4. Preferred employers understand that what is good for society is also good for business. This is an area where our industry is truly world-class. I have witnessed many examples of firms sacrificing profits to "do the right thing" for society as a whole. If your firm isn't willing to do this, you will likely become a recruiting pool for your competitors who do.

5. Preferred employers keep their hiring standards tight. You would never think of waiting until you run out of work on your current projects before marketing new ones. But that's exactly how most firms do their recruiting— they wait until they need people, then start looking for them. When they can't find good ones right away (which is the norm these days), they respond by lowering their standards. After a while, the situation is so desperate that anyone who has a decent resume and can fog a mirror during the interview gets a job offer. Does your firm have a reactive recruiting process like this or are you actively seeking top-notch people all the time?

Firms like Willmer Engineering in Atlanta have seen major benefits from the "hiring slow" approach, where job candidates are thoroughly assessed on their capabilities and personality characteristics and interviewed by potential managers as well as peers. Finally, the firm makes reference checks and speaks to at least one former employer about the candidate's performance.

6. Preferred companies are profitable and growing. You're probably feeling pretty good about this one because your firm has likely been profitable and growing for the past couple of years. But recognize that the entire industry has been growing in both revenues and profitability for the past few years. If your firm isn't growing at least as fast as the overall industry, you are losing ground to your competitors.

Finally, make the employee responsible for primary training. All of these tasks provide wonderful opportunities for your recent grads to dabble in hiring and leadership at an early age, and it is a great way to leverage your firm's resources.

Tip #2: Make it an honor. As the team leader, sit down with your first semester co-ops over lunch, and make it competitive. Let them know you can't hire all the graduates from this program, but you will be hiring the very best. It is in your best interest to make it an honor to be selected for full-time employment in your organization. If you succeed, then the new co-ops will see it from the quality of people executing tip #1, and tip #2 will become a self-fulfilling prophecy.

> *Make it an honor to be selected for full-time employment in your organization.*

Tip #3: Use as a marketing tool. One of our firm's markets is colleges and universities. We have found that developing a strong relationship with a university co-op program can help us win future work. Selection committees often include trustee members. These are "big picture" people who understand the value your company adds through this partnership to the overall value being offered to high-quality student candidates, in which they are increasingly competing for with other institutions.

There is a natural desire to team with consultants who are also helping you achieve your goals. Plus— as a side benefit— students love to work on the very campus they call home. It gives them both a sense of pride and ownership.

Tip #4: Never guarantee the next rotation. It is a mistake to promise three semesters, or feel like you owe three semesters to any co-op student. A co-op program is a long-term investment and real dividends will not be seen for 5 to

10 years. Therefore, if a co-op student does not convince you and your team of his/her potential over the long haul, encourage the person to continue the program with a different type of company for diversity of experience the next semester and reload the pipeline with a new candidate.

Ultimately, this is in the best interest of your firm and the unproductive co-op students. If you have created the right environment and they are not responding, it is an indication they have not yet reached the maturity level needed or your firm is not a good fit for them. Either way, it is better for them to see other opportunities which may spark their creative juices and passion than to flounder for two more semesters.

POTENTIAL HESITATIONS

The following questions are some of the common concerns raised by firms interested in co-op programs:

"What do we do if we don't have a college with a good engineering program nearby?" This is a reasonable concern, but can actually work in your favor. The students who grow up in your geographical region and choose to pursue engineering degrees must have one or two universities they normally select. Often, they would prefer to return home for their co-op experience and want to return home for permanent employment. This combination provides a competitive advantage to you in competing for talent.

"What if I don't have time to train them?" Nothing makes my blood boil more than this attitude. Many years ago, I had a colleague of similar age who was constantly complaining about his workload and inability to find good help. I mentioned the early success our team was experiencing with the co-op program. He responded that he did not have time to train co-ops. He wanted a quick fix.

Years later, the same peer, in the same unchanging situation, asked if he could transfer one of the long-term products of our co-op program into his team. In his words: "If I only had this guy working for me, I could really reduce and manage my workload better." He's still looking for that quick fix. Remember, you can't reap the dividends without first having paid the costs. Unless, of course, you're stealing.

"What if I make this investment and they go work for a competitor?" Is this any different than any type of training at any level of the organization? Unfortunately, if this is your concern, you probably have leadership and cultural problems within your organization that are already affecting retention.

Typically, most personalities drawn to our profession like familiarity and loathe change. If you provide a positive co-op experience, and make it an honor to work with your firm, there will be a natural tendency for them to want to return full-time. In our experience, we have yet to have made an offer in which the co-op did not eventually choose to join our team, even though more financially lucrative opportunities existed in the short-term. In fact, the program is over 10 years old and each of those we made an offer to is still with us, thriving in their careers, successfully operating well beyond the experience should allow, and driving our team to higher levels of success each year. Their energy and optimism is contagious.

WINNING THE TALENT WARS

Winning the battle for talent through the co-op program is a long term investment, but it is a battle you cannot afford to lose. So start now and formulate a winning strategy. Based our firm's experience, you will be very pleased with the results.

Recruiting the Best and the Brightest New Grads. The key to hiring top Millennial graduates is to identify them early and recruit them before they graduate. My experience has shown some form of a co-op/intern program will produce the best success rates. However, not all firms have great access to these programs. Even for those that do, sometimes they are not enough to fill the need for talent in a growing organization. When this is the case, remember to be strategic in hiring new graduates.

In today's hot labor market, you may also have to offer them a signing bonus to convince them to join your firm. One firm combined these tactics in a way that effectively shut out the competition from other potential employers. They identified an outstanding student nine months before graduation and offered a signing bonus of $500 per month while still in school in exchange for signing an employment agreement. This had much more impact than waiting until the student got close to graduation because the $500 per month was much more useful while he was still in school. One architect who knew this student commented, "He was serving imported brews at his parties while his buddies could only afford domestic!"

Before pursuing such a program, however, you have to check with your state's labor statues. In some states, this is allowed. In others, it violates employment laws.

Hiring Graduates: How to Pick the Cream of the Crop . So what do you do if you find yourself needing new graduates that have not come through your co-op program? These days, it's tough to find high-quality technical professionals seeking employment. That is why it's more important than ever for design firms to tap into the labor pool of designers who graduate from colleges and universities every year. Many of these graduates stay with the same firm for years and eventually become senior principals.

Follow these tips to improve the effectiveness of your college recruiting program:

Compensation Tactics for Entry-Level Staff

At the 2005 AIA National Convention & Expo in Las Vegas, a panel of industry leaders addressed current compensation issues in architecture firms. AIA Chief Economist Kermit Baker started off the discussion by noting the ongoing problems design firms face. "We've seen healthy gains in architects' compensation over the past decade, but compensation remains a very divisive issue, and a source of concern at all levels within the profession."

This issue is particularly divisive when it comes to young talent. Baker referenced new AIA data that found 40 percent of firms consider compensation to be a major problem for those entering the profession, and a third of those surveyed thought compensation was a greatest concern for entry-level architects (those with up to four years of experience).

Challenges with new staff

Seminar panel member Meg Brown, director of human resources at Perkins & Will, addressed some of the problems design firms face regarding entry-level employees, and offered advice for overcoming these issues.

Problem: Many firms are creating pay equity issues by offering different salaries to staff with similar talents. If your firm is audited, this can lead to "unintentional discrimination" which ends up costing money in back wages.

Solution: "Get creative. Instead of hiring an intern whose pay is out of alignment with the peer group, perhaps you can give them a signing bonus instead, or give them an early performance review. You will pay a price later on if you hire someone with higher starting wages than the wages of the employees' peers."

Problem: Many young staff are not inclined to see registration as a priority. Architecture firms are contributing to this problem because they are allowing registration to slip among younger employees. While many firms have made a big push for LEED accreditation, they have not pushed for registration.

Solution: "Tie registration to the career path. Expect a return for your investment: let certain staff know that registration is expected if they want early advancement, raises, bonuses, etc."

Problem: Young staff want exciting projects, but they don't want to commit to long-term assignments. There is always excitement on the front-end of projects, but that enthusiasm wanes as the project progresses.

Solution: "To keep staff on projects over the history of the project, offer a completion bonus to award them at the end of the project. This may be decided on a project-by-project basis."

Problem: Staff members recognize they are marketable and can find a new job at any given time.

Solution: "Pay attention to exit interviews. The vast majority of people who leave firms— especially young employees— are not leaving because of money. You need to focus on nonmonetary issues such as communication and firm culture issues."

Problem: Staff want more training and development, not just in hard skills, but in soft skills like marketing. This raises the question: will the increased investment in training yield long-term commitment from the employee, or are you simply training employees for the next employer?

Solution: "Invest in mentoring. Consider 'shadowing,' where you pair your top young talent with a person they can learn from. Allow interns to follow mentors to client meetings. This type of setup helps young people feel like they are getting in on a piece of the action, and lets them see how the firm's work helps the client."

---

1. Recruit early. Start seeking outstanding Millennials at least one year before they graduate. Sharp students used to get offers for employment sometime early in their last semester of college. With the tightening labor market, they now usually get offers two semesters prior to graduation. In the future, the lead time between graduation and when the would-be graduate starts receiving offers is expected to grow.

2. Go for the cream of the crop. Be highly selective when recruiting new grads. Focus not only on students with a good academic record, but also on those with excellent communication skills and a great work ethic. If you hire new grads with these traits, you can teach them everything else they'll need to learn.

3. Don't attend university job fairs. The objective of universities at these job fairs is to place *all* their students. That's different from your objective— hiring only the best and brightest. These students usually don't show up at job fairs because they have a job lined up before graduation.

4. Keep in touch with your former professors. The best way to identify the top talent is to call one of your former professors twice a year and ask, "Do you have any really outstanding students graduating this year?" Your personal relationship with the professor helps you cut through the usual university rhetoric that says: "All of our students are outstanding."

5. Multiply your efforts. Get all your senior staff members to keep in touch with one of their former professors twice a year. If they all do this, you'll have a steady stream of outstanding resumes.

6. Recruit masters. Recruit at the master's rather than the bachelor's level. Firms that do so tell us the learning curve to get new grads productive is far shorter. And the difference in salary is relatively small.

Six Habits of Highly Effective Recruiting. If a co-op/intern program is the best method, and hiring out of school is the first fallback to recruiting high performance Millennials, what happens when you cannot find enough of them to keep up with the company's growth? You have to recruit Millennials already in the workforce. They may be at a competitor or even a client or they have begun their career in the A/E field at all.

Interestingly enough, you still have many opportunities to identify and recruit them. Why? The first few years out of school are a time when people often move around for various reasons.

Hiring Out of School: Is There a Benefit?

Many managers ask for higher qualifications than positions call for, and hire younger, slightly under-qualified candidates who might cost less, and may be more challenged, motivated, and appreciative.

Think outside the box when formulating a hiring strategy. One A/E firm CEO refused to even consider hiring someone straight out of college because of their lack of experience and "real-world" understanding. He relented only because of the serious crunch on talent available to A/E firms.

He has been pleasantly surprised. He has found that Millennials have assimilated into the firm's culture rapidly, have been able to share their technical knowledge (specifically in IT) with the experienced staff, and have also served as "recruitment posters" for more outstanding right-out-of-school talent.

In fact, two of the stars on our team both came to us for the same reason. They graduated from schools in different states, one in Pennsylvania and one in Florida, but were engaged to be married to people who lived in our area. This is not uncommon for this stage of life and gives us a significant opportunity to build our team and thus should not be overlooked as part of your human resource strategy. In fact, one of them was working as an engineer in the manufacturing industry. He has, however, had no difficulty making the transition.

HOW DO THE PROS MANAGE THEIR RECRUITMENT PRACTICES?

1. Sell your company. In Chapter 3, I described the type of culture that attracts star Millennials. During the recruiting process, you must SELL, SELL, SELL that culture! A recruiting culture is a selling culture. The interview can become an inquisition rather than an opportunity to sell the best people on your firm.

You are promoting your firm and the advantages of working with your team, so stress these benefits to the interviewee. And point out that you recognize the value they would bring to your firm.

The interview itself needs to be a balance of profile analysis and selling. If the candidate screening was performed properly upfront, then the face-to-face interview must emphasize selling to attract "the best and the brightest." We will explore this in greater detail in the next chapter.

2. Get key employees recruiting. Principals, office managers, business development leaders, and senior project managers should always be recruiting.

They must look for talent at conferences, on airplanes, with clients, and wherever the opportunity presents itself. On your projects, contractors and subcontractors all represent potential future resources.

3. Don't stop at 5 p.m. Recruiting is a round-the-clock effort. The best don't want to be bothered during the day. They have a good job, and they are giving their all to their employers. Telephone screening interviews often need to be done after-hours.

4. Use your best to recruit the best. People who have enthusiasm, energy, enjoy their job, and are really good at what they do will impress recruits. Interviewees will see who they can learn from if they join the firm and will be favorably impressed.

The best source for finding top-notch Millennials comes from your current staff. If you don't believe it, do a little math. Estimate the number of people your average employee knows in this industry, then multiply by the number of employees.

While most firms encourage their employees to refer their friends to the firm— and some even pay recruiting bonuses— most firms screw up the details, thus rendering their efforts only marginally effective. Here's how to do it right:

Step 1. Don't be cheap! How much do you spend in newspaper ads trying to get decent resumes? How much do you pay a professional recruiter for each new hire?

Here are some suggested minimum amounts you should offer employees for successful referrals:

* Any employee at any level: $1,000
* Employee with a degree in an applicable field: $2,000
* Licensed professional: $3,000

Don't send out a memo telling people you are going to pay them $1,000 and then give them a check for $670. Make the amount net after withholding.

Step 2. Forget the probation period. Most firms wait three to six months before paying the recruiting bonus in case the referred employee doesn't work out. Over 95 percent of new employees referred by

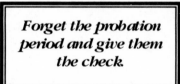

Forget the probation period and give them the check.

current employees make it through the probation period. So forget the probation period and give them the check.

Step 3. Make it a celebration! Most firms just give the employee a check for the referral fee and that's that. Why keep it a secret? Instead, call an all-hands meeting on the first day that the new employee shows up to work, introduce the new employee to the staff, hand out the referral check and ask everyone to applaud the efforts of the recipient in helping bring new talent into the firm.

GO FURTHER

If these ideas aren't creative enough for you, here's one from a firm in Maryland. At the company's Christmas party each year, the firm offers a prize for the employee who recruited the most new employees. The prize is a set of keys on a one-year lease to a new BMW. It costs the firm about $7,000 for this lease (about half the cost of hiring one design professional through a professional recruiter).

The biggest benefit to this is the psychological impact: every time the employee comes to the office and parks that nice, shiny new BMW in the company parking lot, everyone who sees it is reminded of the importance (and personal benefits) of recruiting. And after about six months of driving the BMW, the employee (and his/her spouse) aren't all that eager to go back to their old Ford Taurus. So the firm reports a significant number of repeat winners.

Paint an Accurate Picture of Your Firm to Prospective Employees. Creating an environment in which top talent thrives is re-examined here specifically from the perspective of how it impacts the retention and performance of your top talent. This applies to your firm whether you are hiring in school, upon graduation, or beyond.

1. Firms "oversell" to prospective employees. Overselling anything often comes back to bite us, but perhaps never more than when overselling to prospective employees who quickly discover what it is really like to work for your firm. If it's different from what you portrayed, the trust that is fundamental to inspire an employee's best work has been compromised before you even begin. The bigger the disparity between how you portray your organization and their actual experience, the less likely they are to apply their best efforts to your firm.

2. You can't accurately portray what you don't understand. Many A/E firms don't really have a solid understanding of their own culture from the employees' perspective. In many cases, management has been significantly surprised by some findings that emerge from this process. In many cases, the issue was plain to see, but management wasn't looking— or listening, such as during exit interviews with disgruntled employees who are leaving. In retrospect, how many of your employees that didn't work out were just fundamentally incompatible with your organization, and on a trajectory for this unfortunate ending right from the start?

OVERCOMING THE CHALLENGE

A firm suffered from high employee turnover and a demoralized workforce as employees grew frustrated with the last-minute culture of the organization and the anxiety it created. The principals were concerned that they had a culture that didn't foster happy, long-term employees. The objective is not to change their culture, but rather do a better job of communicating their culture to prospective employees— to communicate the "pending reality" of what it would be like to work there.

The partners began to include "explanations" in interviews with prospective employees, such as; "You know, we have somewhat of a last-minute culture around here. We meet our commitments to our clients, but we frequently burn the midnight oil when we are coming up on a deadline and things can get pretty frenetic. So, if this is the type of environment that energizes you— great, let's talk further— but if not, well, it's better that we bring it up now."

Should You Hire an In-House Recruiter?

When I ask managers in design firms about their experiences in using recruiting firms (aka headhunters) to help them deal with shortages of employees, I inevitably get two responses: bad and very bad.

The costs for using recruiters is very high (generally 20 to 35 percent of the employee's first year's salary), and the quality of candidates is highly variable.

Does that mean you should forget about using professional recruiters and just go back to the old methods, like running ads in the local paper? Perhaps not.

Consider another alternative: hiring professional recruiters as employees, rather than using them on a success-fee basis. A large West Coast engineering firm used this approach to cope with a 25-percent-per-year sales growth and the resulting demand for more manpower. They hired an individual who had many years' experience as a professional recruiter and really knew how to dig out top talent.

His duties were as follows:

* Developing and placing national employment advertising
* Facilitating/coordinating the communication of employment needs and potential candidates between offices, including transmittal of resumes and setting up interviews at the various offices
* Distributing resumes to offices for consideration
* Screening candidates on behalf of office managers by reviewing resumes and conducting screening interviews where appropriate
* Assisting office managers, when requested, in placing offers of employment, confirming starting salary and relocation terms, and administering other front-end employment actions
* Working with office managers to improve the quality and effectiveness of recruiting methods and materials
* Expediting the college recruiting program
* Coordinating recruiting efforts at national trade shows

> The prime responsibility for recruiting and hiring remained with the profit and cost center managers; the recruiter was simply provided by the home office as a resource to aid in these efforts.
>
> The results of this position were excellent; the recruiter was able to place more than 300 employees over a period of four years.
>
> The cost for the professional recruiter was about $120,000 per year including salary, benefits, travel costs, and administrative support. This sum was a fraction of what it would have cost the firm to have placed these new employees under the traditional success-fee arrangement. And more important, the recruiter's loyalties were to the firm, not to a quota he had to meet in order to get his bonus from a headhunting firm.
>
> If your firm is too small to justify the costs of a full-time in-house recruiter, consider connecting with other firms to jointly fund such a position. For example, if yours is an architectural firm, you might consider sharing this expense with several of the subconsultants you regularly use.

This scenario is a good example of a situation in which both factors described above came into play. The partners hadn't exactly been broadcasting their last-minute style, and they really didn't understand the full impact it was having on creating an environment in which people are motivated to do their best work. This small shift in approach was pivotal in helping them overcome their turnover and cultural challenges and allowed prospective employees to sort themselves in or out based on a real understanding of the culture of the organization.

You may be thinking that it sounds crazy to "scare off" potential employees, but ultimately you won't benefit from hiring people who don't work out. Remember, hiring them— convincing someone to join your firm— is actually the easy part. The hard part is delivering on the promises you make (or imply) during your pre-hire presentation. When you consider the cost of hiring and rehiring, and the impact that underperformers (let alone flatly disgruntled employees) have on the rest of the office, it's best to let the incompatible ones get away— even the talented ones.

I recently asked the Millennials on our team what it was that we communicated during the interview process that made them want to join the team. They gave a list of reasons, all of which were outlined in Chapter 3. Then I asked them an even more important question "How well did we live up to what was advertised?" I was not sure what they would say, but their answers were very satisfying. To a person, they said during the interview they all found it difficult to believe we were really the kind of place we were selling. Seemed too good to be true. However, after joining the team, they all found we were even better. Now, that's certainly more than expected and right where I want us to be. Just as with marketing to clients, in marketing to Millennial candidates, always undersell and over-deliver.

The challenge for me and the rest of the team will be to continue to hit this target in the future. Asking the people who recently joined your team is the best way to measure how well you are doing. If not, we may find ourselves eventually 'drinking our own Kool-Aid.'

Onboarding: It Takes a Year to Do It Right

Once you've recruited a Millennial, your job is not done, but has only just begun. Do not forget to be strategic in 'onboarding' the Millennial, the process of integrating them into the firm. Successful onboarding begins with all-important first impressions, and can be structured to make hiring and initial welcome an extension of the recruiting process. Cheryl May, the director of strategic leadership development at the Advanced Management Institute for Architecture and Engineering, shares the following advice:

Employee and particularly potential future rainmaker turnover can be one of the most expensive costs a firm can experience. Authorities widely estimate that the cost of replacing a professional can equal one years' salary and benefits, with a corresponding six-month cost for someone in a non-professional role.

When there is a shortage of qualified professionals-- as currently being experienced in the A/E industry-- losses can be even higher. What can you do to make sure that when you hire someone they will feel at home quickly, become productive as soon as possible, and become a valued part of your firm's "family"-- experiencing personal and career fulfillment and developing a commitment to stay for the long term?

Whether your first contact with a prospective employee is a want ad, your web site, a phone call, or simply your firm's reputation in the community, how you first respond to a person can determine whether he or she wants to work in your firm or not.

Among these many initial contact opportunities are your firm's application form, a referral by an employee, an on-campus recruiting effort, an internship, or for more experienced professionals, working on a project team together. Keep in mind that how your firm responds to first contacts can also includes the lack of a response. If you never return that first call, or e-mail, or follow up on an introduction, you're sending out a negative message about your firm. And people will tell others 'I never heard back from them.'

Onboarding is often an awkward time; after the "romance" of the interview process is over, comes the struggle to become comfortable in a new job and with new colleagues. The Society for Human Resource Management says that 70% of all new employees are sent home the first day because the organization was not prepared for them. Another often-quoted statistic is that the highest turnover rate is within the first 90 days of employment.

Some firms find ways to give prospective employees a feeling for the company's culture and whether they'd fit in, such as a "Wall of Employees" with a photo of each person holding up an object that has personal meaning for them. Others include a photo wall, but with pictures from every company event-- softball games, awards, birthdays, and other milestones. These firms have placed the pictures in highly visible spots, and make sure that prospects have time to look them over during the recruiting process. Terracon Consulting Engineers literally gives new employees the "Red Carpet Treatment," with a crimson carpet leading into their office, not only to welcome them, but to provide a visual cue to everyone to stop in and welcome the new employee.

Terracon also assigns an ambassador, charged with filling the new person in on those elusive, informal processes that aren't documented in the company manual-- how to use the Intranet, who to ask for various kinds of help, etc. The ambassador and new hire meet every other week for 90 days, so there is a scheduled time to review questions as they come up, and the new employee always has someone to ask for help.

Other firms emphasized that feeling welcomed and wanted on the first day can be as simple as finding your new desk stocked with business cards, a welcome sheet with log-in info for voicemail, computer and e-mail, or finding that your first e-mail links to a web page with photos of everyone in the firm. For new employees of larger firms, it can be daunting to learn a large roster of names and faces, so this kind of online directory can be very effective for telling the CEO from the CFO at the "welcome aboard" lunch.

From the first introduction to your firm to the day when an employee finally feels like "part of the family" usually takes a full year. The year offers you many opportunities to let them know they're wanted, and to engage them for the long term-- and employee engagement is the key to career-long retention.

Special onboarding processes are needed for younger generations. It is particularly important for Millennials to create meaning in their work early on. They value the history of the company and want to know how they fit in, and why their work has meaning in the larger scheme.

One firm respond to this issue by sending young rainmakers, managers, and directors to a retreat where they have 90 minutes to build a bicycle, create a marketing plan, and sell it to the facilitator. They are then asked, "How would you feel if your work was to assemble these bicycles all day, every day?" Most of them don't find that terribly appealing, until the second question engenders a sense of purpose: "What if all those bikes you built were going to kids who couldn't otherwise have a bike?"

Holidays Are a Perfect Time for Recruiting

A thorough strategic plan should have a section dedicated to hiring and recruiting for next year. Whether your growth and personnel needs are great or slight, now is the time to take a proactive approach to recruiting.

The end of the year is an ideal time for candidates to explore new opportunities. Projects are wrapping up, vacation time has to be used, and New Year's resolutions are being pondered. How many times during the holidays do we hear our friends and family members say that they "seriously need a career boost" in the next year?

This is a great time to show Millennials already in our industry that your firm can offer them better opportunities, more growth, better benefits, or whatever appeals to them. Now is the time to fill next year's critical needs before they become too critical and you end up losing out on new business due to lack of staffing. We have all been guilty of waiting too long to look for a new or replacement employee, and end up regretting it after a hot project comes along. That's when you can't get an employee in your door fast enough, and too often you lose the project.

Put your feelers out as soon as possible. The holidays are a great time to do this because everybody spirits are up, and you run into plenty of candidates every day. Next time you are at an association party (and if you are not a member of a professional association, stop reading and sign up), take a look around the room. I bet that at least half of the people there are potential talent for your firm. Talk to them— not necessarily about a job, but talk to them about your firm, the exciting projects you are bidding on, the growth potential for the firm, your talented employees and interesting work (bring a mid-level staffer to attest to this).

Though the holidays are a great time to meet potential recruits, convincing somebody to make a move during this season is challenging. I suggest using the following strategies to attract new employees in the new year:

1. Talk to your contacts about their careers and their jobs. Offer your business card and an invitation for them to stop by "just to chat" anytime they are in the neighborhood. You will be surprised at how many will follow through and meet with you— better the candidates come to you than you go searching for them!

2. Offer a sign-on bonus. People stand to lose a lot— their end-of-the-year bonus— should they change jobs before January 1. The amount can range from $1,000 to over $50,000. On the lower end of this scale, this worry can be alleviated with a sign-on that is comparable to their end-of-the-year bonus.

3. Set a start date after January. Let the candidate collect his or her bonus for the work they did in the last year. This also allows the candidate to not upset his or her life too much with making a move near the holidays when they probably already have scheduled time off, and are used to how holiday periods work at their current firm. Get an offer out now, and have them sign it.

4. Expand your holiday party list. Invite candidates that you have been speaking with to your company party. This is a terrific way to get them to meet your firm, get a feel for the people and your culture, and create professional friendships that will help them make the decision to join your firm.

Set the groundwork now, and you'll be able to have key new staff members ready to help your firm grow next year.

Finding and Keeping Qualified A/E Professionals

Peter Ashton Lyon is chief marketing officer with U.S. COST, Inc. and offers the following advice:

Finding and keeping qualified professionals is a major concern of business leaders in the A/E industry. Recruiting qualified, skilled personnel has become so critical to the life of a firm that filling key positions has become an integral part of many A/E firm's business plans and strategic marketing plans.

The reasons for this phenomenon are two-fold. There are fewer young people entering careers in the built environment, and existing, experienced professionals are retiring and leaving the industry.

Enrollments in architectural schools is decreasing and even though there is an increase in young people seeking engineering degrees, they are moving away from the built environment into other more lucrative technical fields. Architecture and engineering in the built environment is simply not paying the starting salaries of other industries.

To combat this trend, A/E industry leaders are thinking outside the box to find, hire, train and keep qualified professionals. Creative and innovative approaches are being developed, which center on the following key company initiatives.

Building a recruitment culture within the firm. The leadership and commitment to building a recruiting culture within a firm must come directly from the top. The firm's leadership must create the environment that promotes education and advancement not only for the firm's existing and new staff members, but also for young people who are considering entering the industry.

Several strategies to use include:

* Allowing senior technical staff with paid leave to teach at local colleges and technical schools.
* Forming partnerships with college/technical school deans by sponsoring academic events, competitions, and providing mentoring opportunities for students, and promoting staff involvement in these programs.
* Making recruitment activities a part of every employee's performance review.
* Integrating marketing and human resources into a team effort to secure skilled, qualified personnel.

This positive recruitment culture works to secure skilled staff members for the firm. It also serves to keep valued professional staff members with the firm.

Recruiting at colleges, universities, and technical schools. Identifying and securing qualified professionals requires a planned, proactive approach. The company culture and top-leadership support and encouragement give creditability to this planned approach. Approaches used for universities and technical schools include:

* Participating in school sponsored job fairs.
* Creating design and/or engineering design competitions.
* Creating internship opportunities for rising third and fourth year students.
* Sponsoring lunch-and-learn technical events at the office for student organizations and the classes.
* Allowing university/technical school alumni organizations to use the company's facilities for meetings.
* Offering significant scholarships ($10,000 plus) to deserving third year students in the disciplines needed.
* Collecting permanent phone numbers of graduating seniors and following up with a phone call to the family home after five years to inquire about their success in the industry. (Strategy: The student, after five years, is trained and may be ready to move up.)
* Creating a monthly newsletter outlining the staff resources needed and distribute the newsletter internally and externally to local college/technical school professors and industry organizations.

To effectively work industry/trade organizations, several ideas include:

* Allowing technical staff members to present technical papers and/or make presentations at organization meetings.
* Sponsoring events that allow firm leaders to distribute company literature and/or profile the firm during organization meetings.
* Placing classified or display page advertising in professional organization's publications.
* Incorporating internet/web site recruiting through search engines as well as through the company web site.

CHAPTER 6

Strategic Interviewing

"Hope is not a strategy."
> – Dr. John Maxwell, leadership trainer

When talking with principals across the country, they often share some of the problems their firms are experiencing. Two of the common ones are: "We can't find enough good people," or "Our people want to be partners and owners, but we can't get them to show any motivation." The list goes on.

When confronted with these issues, I always start with the same question. "What is your strategy to address this problem?" By their answer, I can immediately tell if principals have any strategy at all, or even worse, they believe circumstances are beyond their control and they are 'victims.' The very first step, in which there is no shortcut, on the path to becoming an effective leader is to take responsibility for your situation. Leaders are never 'victims.'

There is one word I listen for that, if used in their response to my question, is a clear indication they are not thinking strategically. That word is "HOPE." "We can't find enough good people," they say. "OK, what is your strategy to find more good people?" I ask. "Well," they continue, "we are HOPING that we'll get some better resumes soon."

Hope is not a strategy!

While hope is a good thing in life, it has nothing to do with being strategic! A great place to apply this principle is in your interviewing strategy. That's right; you should have an interviewing plan and strategy. The goal of strategic interviewing is two-fold. First, you want to separate the wheat from the chaff. You want to have a high probability of identifying those individuals who will thrive in your firm, help you fulfill the vision of the firm, add value, and be a joy to work with. Bringing the wrong people into the firm hurts us in three critical ways:

1. We invest a lot of time in training them which is money down the drain.
2. The time they are with us delays us from searching for and finding the right person.
3. It de-motivates and drains our existing staff.

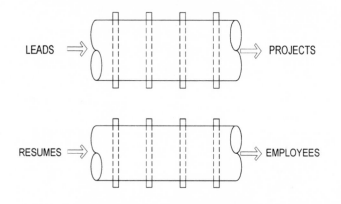

> **The more time you spend hiring the right people, the less time you will spend managing them!**

Second, once we have identified the right person, we want to SELL them on the firm. As mentioned previously, this more often than not means we are competing for their services much like we compete for projects.

Most firms take a very haphazard approach to interviewing. It's almost an afterthought, something firm principals are required to be involved in that is a distraction from their more 'urgent' tasks. Unfortunately, this not only reduces our chances of identifying the right person but it also communicates to them we do not have our act together. As a result, the majority of candidates that accept our offer are not the cream of the crop. If they were, some other more strategic thinking firm would have most likely secured their services.

So, how do we become strategic in our interviewing? Let's break it down into two sections. First, tips for identifying the right candidate through the interview process. Second, how to sell them on the firm and close the deal.

TO HIRE MORE PEOPLE, INTERVIEW FEWER CANDIDATES

Most A/E firms interview too many candidates. When done correctly, this is enormously time-consuming for the staff who have to conduct the interviews and record the results. By the time you invite a candidate to your office for an interview, you should be 90 percent sure that you will make an offer. And if you conduct the process properly, 90 percent of the candidates you interview will accept your offer. It all begins with strategically defining the job description.

Step 1: The job description. Too often this is an afterthought that receives minimal attention as we wrestle with our other daily challenges. "Just put down an electrical PE with 5 to 25 years experience," we tell the HR director. If you want to attract the most appropriate prospective applicants, however, start with a job description that describes to a "T" the position your organization seeks to fill.

> *Start with a job description that describes to a "T" the position your organization seeks to fill.*

Also, always be on the lookout for talent from unique sources. In one situation, an individual working for a well-respected design firm wrote an article in a publication that happened to be exactly what another firm's hiring manager needed to win a client. The hiring manager contacted the author and offered him a job after a brief interview session at the client's office.

Step 2: Screening. The next step is to screen the resumes. The objective of this screening is to eliminate candidates who have a low probability of becoming all-stars.

Things to look for are:

* **Evidence of carelessness, for example, typos.** If the person does not care enough to proof a resume, it's a good indication of an overall lack of attention to detail.
* **A poorly written cover letter.** The ability to write well is a hallmark of almost every successful design professional.
* **A hard-to-follow resume.** This is a sign of a disorganized mind.
* **A record of frequent job changes.** If a candidate has changed jobs every one to two years during a 15-year career, there is probably a reason. However, this does not likely apply to Millennials.

When looking at the resumes of Millennials, look for clues to potential leadership ability. Have they been the leader of a non-profit organization? Does any of their previous work experience suggest a strong work ethic?

Depending upon the position, HR may be inundated with hundreds of resumes. In some instances, HR relies on software to help narrow down the field of resumes using keywords that the hiring manager has specified to qualify the resumes that will be reviewed further. HR should not stop there, but make it part of their review to scan the applicant's cover letter or introduction. In a profession such as consulting, HR staffers need to "drill down" and closely evaluate the projects the applicant lists— these could be valuable nuggets of information that can provide marketing insight.

Step 3: Telephone interviews. The next step is to conduct a 15- to 30-minute telephone interview. The objective of this interview is to further screen candidates who aren't able to communicate effectively over the phone or who don't seem to fit with your firm.

The agenda for the phone interview should include:

* Thanking the person for submitting a resume
* Finding out why the person is interested in changing jobs, if applicable, and interested in your firm in particular
* If they are just entering the workforce, determining why are they interested in the AEC industry
* Determining what the candidate liked and disliked about previously held positions
* Asking about geographic preferences

When you find a candidate who communicates well and seems to be a good fit for your firm, ask him/her for a copy of a document that he/she has written and the names and phone numbers of at least three professional references.

Now, a word of caution here. You have to consider the age of the person when doing the phone interview, but not in a discriminatory way. As an example, 10 years ago when I was recruiting our first co-op candidate, I also followed these three steps. However, during the phone interview with one candidate, right in the middle of the conversation, he said, "Hold on a minute, somebody just beeped in" and the phone went silent.

I looked at the phone in disbelief for a moment wondering if what just happened really happened. About a minute later, he beeped back in and we completed the interview. In spite of what had occurred, he was the most promising candidate so I made him an offer.

Today, this engineer leads one of our most promising opportunities and has been a go-to guy for years. Clients love him, co-workers love him, and he has a bright future. I do not, however, ever let him forget about that phone interview. It still to this day makes him blush when I bring it up.

The message here is when interviewing Millennials, you have to look beyond some of the things they do that are not "professional." They are not yet professionals and should not be expected to completely act as such.

Step 4: Evaluate work samples and references. The next step is to evaluate the document you receive from the applicant. If it shows good organization and well-presented ideas, call the professional references.

When contacting references, remember, there are only two kinds of responses: glowing and otherwise. Comments that indicate only qualified endorsements or evasive answers to questions are indications of trouble— eliminate the candidate from consideration.

In reality, I have found references given on a resume to be of little value. If they do have any work experience in our industry, however, find someone you or one of your colleagues knows who knows them. Normally, companies can only confirm the dates of their employment. In our lawsuit-happy world, this is all you

> *When contacting references, remember, there are only two kinds of responses: glowing and otherwise.*

can expect. However, if you can talk to someone you know directly, or even indirectly, you can bypass the legalese.

Recently, I received a resume from an individual I knew had worked with a client of mine. The resume looked very promising. However, I decided to give my friend a call first. I called him on his cell phone. He was on vacation skiing in Vermont. "Sorry to bother you," I said, "but I just received a resume from such and such." Without me saying another word, he responded, "I wouldn't hire him if he was the last engineer on the face of the earth." Case closed.

Today, there's another tool to help pre-screen Millennials. A forward-thinking Boomer who leads a large civil engineering firm recently shared it with me. Facebook and MySpace are two social networking web sites aimed at Millennials. A vast majority of Millennials have personal information about them on these web sites available to the public for free and, according to my friend, the information they put on these sites can be very revealing. How about that!

Recently this has been confirmed in the press. Millennials are now just starting to be warned of the danger these web sites pose during the interview process and are being encouraged to 'clean them up.' However, I doubt many Millennials think older generations are smart enough to access these sites. It's another tool to use in prescreening.

By the time a candidate has passed the above screenings, there should be a 90 percent probability that you will make an offer. During the interview, this allows you to focus the effort on selling your firm to the candidate. If you do it right, 90 percent of candidates will accept your offer.

Step 5: Identify an Interview Host. Those A/E firms that successfully recruit valuable and sought-after employees communicate a high level of professionalism both during the interview process and afterwards— and make sure candidates feel they are truly wanted by the firm.

To do so, each interviewee appointment needs a host, someone who will guide them through the process and make them feel at home. This is a critical role, and serves another purpose we will describe later.

One large A/E firm takes a strategic approach by clearly defining the role of the host in order to ensure that priority candidates receive the top-flight treatment that will make them want to join the firm's team. This is their story:

Case Study
Strategic Hosting

A Chicago-based A/E firm appoints a senior-level manager to serve as the "host" for the candidate. This individual is key to creating that all-important "first impression" and must convey an air of professionalism throughout the interview process.

The host begins by making the applicant feel comfortable, and perhaps suggest to the applicant what the initial interview will be like, who the person will meet, and what materials to bring along to share during the interview. Such dialogue helps the applicant feel like he or she is important and makes for a less-intimidating initial interview.

Once a candidate is targeted for an interview, the responsibility for scheduling and designing the interviewing process is assigned to the "host."

The "host" should possess the following qualities:
* Have at least four years of experience with the firm if possible, but should also be as close in age to the candidate as practical
* Be an ardent supporter of the firm
* Have a personal interest in recruiting other top-notch people
* Have an experience level similar to the candidate
* Be well versed in the firm's culture and business and be knowledgeable about all its clients and projects

This firm has the "host" manager take the following steps:
1. Personally contact the candidate to confirm interview arrangements.
2. Ensure that all travel plans are handled properly and communicated to the candidate.
3. Meet out-of-town candidates at the airport or train station and drive them to the office.
4. See that an appropriate package of company materials— with a cover letter— is sent out to the candidate in advance of the interview.
5. Ask the candidate to fill out an application before the interview.
6. Develop an agenda that is agreed upon by the appropriate managers.
7. Send the agenda to the candidate in advance of the interview so that he/she knows what to expect that day.
8. Communicate with all staff members who will be involved in the interview process to ensure that each one is available and familiar with the schedule and the candidate's qualifications.

9. Meet with all of the interviewers to make sure that each one knows his/her role in the interview process. This step helps to avoid having the candidate answer the same questions from seven different interviewers.
10. Escort the candidate through the day, attempting to keep to the schedule as closely as possible.

If the other interviews have gone well, the last stop should be with the CEO or the most senior individual in the office. This particular interview is the most essential one.

The CEO's role is to sell the firm. A strong pitch by the head person in the organization is one of the most important factors when high-quality candidates determine which offer to accept.

After the interviews, the host:
1. Holds a relaxed lunch with several other staff members— not the interviewers— who speak knowledgeably and favorably about the firm and the area.
2. Conducts a tour of the office and, when feasible, visits a nearby project site.
3. Arranges for some sightseeing and other activities designed to present the city in a favorable light for out-of-town candidates.
4. Makes sure that all interviewers document their discussions with the candidate.
5. Ensures that reimbursement of the candidate's travel expenses is handled promptly.
6. Sends an immediate thank-you letter to the candidate, and lets him/her know the time frame for decision-making. Stays in touch with the candidate until a decision is made.
7. Finally, and perhaps most important, the host manager ensures that a timely decision is made and that follow-up is handled in such a manner that the candidate will either accept the firm's offer or feel positive about the firm even if an offer is not made.

This successful A/E firm offers some final advice about conducting interviews:
* Make sure follow-up procedures are handled professionally with every interviewee. Unprofessional follow-up after a candidate has taken the time to interview with you is sure to earn the firm a black eye.

The host plays an important role in a successful interview strategy. Find the right person to serve this role for each potential target.

When recruiting Millennials out of college, or as co-op/intern students, there are advantages to using someone closer to the candidate's age as the host, versus a senior professional. Besides the obvious benefit from resource utilization, this person can help communicate why your firm is a great place for Millennials to work.

Either way, the host plays an important role in a properly developed recruiting strategy.

Step 6: Interview Strategy. If you have completed the steps above, there should already be increased odds by the time of the in office interview that you have identified the right candidate. However, this is still the most important step in making this decision. It is also the last step. Before the interview day is complete, you should have your mind made up. The morning of the interview is about making this determination.

> *Finding the right person for the job has morphed into a skill that requires extreme diligence and research.*

In today's highly competitive workplace, whether in the architectural, engineering or design field, finding the right person for the job has morphed into a skill that requires extreme diligence and research. Listening attentively and fielding poignant questions can make the difference, and throwing in a little courtesy and professional respect adds a classy touch.

Here are a few suggestions:

The task of prepping for an interview isn't just for the applicants; interviewers can gain much from scrutinizing applicants' resumes just before the interview. Many open-ended questions can spring from the information the applicant has laid before you.

The interview. An interview is not about one side doing all the talking. Rather, it's an open dialogue that should flow smoothly, with the interviewer leading with open-ended questions and allowing the applicant to describe his or her core competencies, soft skills, and strengths.

In reality, too many HR and hiring managers fail to zero-in on some key points the applicant may be making, or worse, take copious notes during the interview and fail to brief the other managers in the food chain about what the interviewee said. Nothing turns a prospective employee off more than to realize that a hiring manager or HR person has not listened to the applicant nor taken them seriously.

As previously mentioned, if your recruiting includes a careful screening and interviewing process, you should be right more than 95 percent of the time. Hiring right the first time takes more effort, but the payback is tremendous.

To hire right the first time, you must be strategic in planning and preparing for interviews. When interviewing candidates, you want to ask applicants open-ended questions that can't be simply answered with a "Yes" or "No." Here are some examples:

1. What do you know about architecture and engineering and the position you are interviewing for?
2. What would you change about your current job?
3. What are you looking for in your next job?
4. What are the personal qualities this job demands?
5. What are your strengths?
6. Tell me how you react to a crisis situation? (Give an example)
7. Have you ever worked for more than one manager?
8. How does your job relate to the overall success of your department and your company?
9. What special responsibilities outside your regular duties have you been given?

10. Tell me about an occasion when you chose, for whatever reason, not to finish a particular task.
11. Describe what you think a typical day is like on this job.
12. What kind of work interests you the most?
13. How would you define a successful career?
14. Describe your method of keeping track of important matters.
15. How do you plan your day?
16. How would you plan for a major project?
17. When have you rescheduled your time to accommodate an unexpected workload?
18. How will you establish a working relationship with the employees in this company?
19. How would you work with the various different opinions in a team in order to reach a goal?
20. What skills can you bring to this position, other than the ones required in the job description?
21. How do you get along with people that you don't like?
22. How do you take criticism?

Right after the interview, fill out the rating form. You should determine the dividing line between a satisfactory and unsatisfactory candidate in advance, based on the requirements of the opening. One or two circles in the unsatisfactory area might rule a candidate out.

Hiring Takes More than Gut Instincts. A mistake we all make is to become infatuated with a candidate early after introductions. Particularly in this robust economy we desperately want to fill the most needed positions, and when a person shows up with charisma, energy, and the ability to tell us what we want to hear, we will tend to justify all the reasons to hire based on our gut (and, too often, our overwhelming need for talent).

Recruiting: Balancing Ethics and Effectiveness

When hiring new employees, most design firms still employ the traditional "they find us" approach. In today's tight labor market, will this strategy continue to be adequate for your firm? Or do you need to adopt some form of the "we find them" approach? If the latter, you will need to define how to balance ethics and effectiveness. Here are some suggestions:

Clarify your firm's ethical boundaries in recruiting. The first step is to assess the ethical consistency of your current practices. For example, firm managers who claim that initiating the pursuit of a competitor's employee is wrong, but yet these firms have no problem hiring an outside recruiter to do the same thing. Plus, they offer referral bonuses to employees who bring candidates to the firm (that are subsequently hired), which would seem to encourage the very behavior they call unethical. So where's the line? It is important to clarify where your firm stands on the ethics of recruiting.

Work within the context of relationships. Is it wrong to recruit a friend? Most would say, typically not. So a starting point in avoiding the ethical quagmire in recruiting from competitors is to work within existing relationships. This is the intended purpose of referral bonuses, to encourage employees to talk to their friends and former colleagues about joining their firm. The "we find them" approach is rooted in relationships. Not only does this address some of the ethical dilemma, but it's a far more effective way to recruit. The "they find us" method attracts mostly strangers, where you have to make a quick assessment of the candidate's competencies and character— leading to more than a few hiring disappointments. Plus recruiting people you know involves less ethical ambiguity than hiring an outside recruiter to steal away someone you don't know from a competitor.

Don't oversell the opportunity. When pursuing an impressive candidate, it's expected that you make your best sales pitch. But in your enthusiasm, don't overlook your duty to try to ensure a good fit. The candidate's credentials may be stellar, but that doesn't necessarily mean he or she is the right person for the job, or vice versa.

This is absolutely the wrong thing to do. While gut is an indication, there are a couple of other tools we should rely on. One tool is scenario interviews to test a candidate's leadership and decision-making skills. Using scenarios during the interview process elicits responses that show how a candidate "thinks on his or her feet," and allows a candidate to demonstrate decision-making strategies that rely on business knowledge and experiential

> *While gut is an indication, there are a couple of other tools we should rely on.*

standing. Getting past asking questions about past experiences by presenting a unique and possibly new situation gives interviewers a better idea of the leadership qualities we all are looking for in today's candidates.

Finally, make sure you have a committee, formal or informal, to discuss a candidate's background and experiences, scenario interview results and references. Haste makes waste: Be patient with the process.

Reveal Your Candidate's Emotional Style. In your next interview, guide the conversation towards personality and ask, "Tell me about a time a co-worker gave you advice." This question will uncover vital information about the candidate:

* **Is the candidate open to criticism or constructive feedback?** Listen closely to the response and hear if the candidate was able to grasp the feedback or if he or she became uncomfortable and defensive.

* **Is the candidate receptive to change?** Did the candidate view the suggestion constructively? If the candidate says that they didn't realize they had that trait, or that they changed the behavior, you can have confidence in their response to future concerns.

* **How independent is the candidate?** The candidate's answer can be interpreted in a number of ways. If they became embarrassed by the advice and wanted to change to fit the role, they may be a follower. If they disagreed with the advice, it could signal an independent, free spirit. Or it could mean they are prideful and vain. Listen closely to the rest of the conversation and put the answers into context.

* **How much do they respect their co-workers?** If they took the advice of their co-worker, it could mean belief in strong ties and the trust that comes from team effort.

Step 7: Be efficient and make a decision. Don't let a good Millennial prospect pass because you hesitate on decisions. The Millennial generation is used to instant responses. If you are strategic in your recruiting, this can be a huge advantage for your firm, because most firms are very slow in their hiring processes. Don't wait too long to have the interviewee come in, or wait too long after the interview to make an offer. Just the fact that you are responsive demonstrates to the potential candidate you know what you want, are decisive, and can get things done.

> *The Millennial generation is used to instant responses.*

The interviewee should know clearly and precisely when he or she will hear back on the decision. It should not be longer than a week and preferably less than two days. For really top-notch candidates, let them know before the day is out.

"How do we know, that quickly?" you may ask. If you have properly pre-screened a potential Millennial, and have strategically executed the interview process, you should know the decision before the interview is over.

You can use your host to help you with this effort. We use the morning part of the interview to determine if they are the right candidate for our team. The host then takes the candidate to lunch. During lunch, we have a chance to caucus with the team and come to a decision.

Whether you plan on hiring an applicant or not, common courtesy dictates you should notify the person within a reasonable time. While your time is valuable, theirs is, too. What firm would you rather be: one that notifies applicants they were not chosen, or one that waits until the applicant makes continued inquires of their status? It takes little effort to notify a person of the outcome, and e-mails are acceptable. That applicant may someday be your next client, or worse, employer. A little common courtesy and respect works wonders.

Step 8: Sell the Firm! If during lunch we decide to make the candidate an offer, then the afternoon is no longer about determining if the candidate is a good fit, it's about SELLING the firm. The candidate, however, is not informed of the switch.

Take them around to meet everyone, especially other Millennials. Let them spend some time with your team and give your team the opportunity to sell your firm. Nothing sells a Millennial like another Millennial telling them the benefits of joining your organization in their own language.

Also, this is the time to really sell the culture. What is it about your firm that Millennials find attractive. Highlight these issues! If you are strategic, these messages will be on the walls of the office already. The interviewee is looking for cultural clues as they wander the office. They pay attention to what the dress code is and don't have to be told. They are taking it all in.

Case Study
The Rewards of "Hiring Slow"

The "hire slow" motto needs to be repeated over and over to keep you focused on hiring people for "careers" as opposed to "jobs." This axiom is difficult any time applied, even more so today with the shortage of engineers in the pool and the myriad of competitors vying for their expertise. When a firm practices in a niche market, the competition for qualified candidates becomes even more intense.

Doris Willmer, president of the Atlanta firm Willmer Engineering, Inc., was introduced to the concept of "hiring slow" through her involvement in a CEO issues roundtable.

"Having gone the route of hiring people that appeared to be a good fit based on an hour interview, acceptable physical presentation during the interview, and tepid references, we had a desire to put additional structure around the hiring process. In order to maximize the benefit of the time spent in the interview process with more probable success of a good hire not only for the company but also for the candidate, we initiated an integrated approach to filling positions with the right people," explains Willmer.

The company's hiring process consists of three major elements— equally weighted— that present a picture of how a candidate may operate in a new corporate environment. Willmer offers an outline of these steps below.

Step 1. The first step in the hiring process involves using an assessment that measures mental capabilities and personality characteristics.

Each item in the assessment is normed based on the attributes that are desired for the position in question. Not all positions require the same attributes, so establishing norms based on national norms or factors that reflect your company's specific culture provide a measurement of how a candidate may fit in your company culture. Of course, to establish the norms internally requires each of your existing employees to participate in the process as well. You can accomplish this with minimal financial investment by creating a focus group within the company to establish norms for each specific position in the firm. The norms can then be adjusted over time as each current employee completes the assessment as part of their annual review.

Once norms for each position are established, candidates can be evaluated against those already functioning successfully within the company. Having the appropriate norms for a position is critical in evaluating the assessment results as well as selecting the measures that are most critical to success in your culture. Management must decide what the most desirable measures are and evaluate the candidate objectively against them. Once you establish these critical factors, each candidate can be evaluated objectively against them.

Step 2. Hold detailed, face-to-face interviews with the candidate and all potential mangers as well as peers. This allows the candidate to get an overall feel for the people they will be working with as well as engages the appropriate staff in the selection process.

Step 3. The third and very critical piece of the process involves a check of references. Many companies have policies that only confirm employment dates or check whether the former employee is eligible for rehire. A thorough reference check will attempt to talk to at least one former employer who will address performance or other issues that are important to the candidate's success at your firm.

Once the assessment, interviews, and reference checks are completed, all persons involved in the interview process should be consulted to review the data and determine if an offer will be made. Each area of the process should be weighted equally, hence one-third weight given to the assessment, interview, and reference checks.

Closer to success

Willmer admits that there is no guarantee that firms will find the best match with every hire, but firms will improve their odds.

"Not all hires are a perfect fit. Even if the process is consistently applied, the same line holds true: 'You never really know someone until you live with them.' However, the process tends to minimize potential disappointments associated with hiring a candidate solely on a good resume and interview. Using the assessment and reference checks as additional tools help make a hire a win-win for the company and the candidate."

Keep in mind, of course, if the decision during lunch is this candidate is not the right fit for the firm, then there is no reason to continue with Step 8. When they get back with the host from lunch, thank them for their time, send them on their way, and tell them you will get back with them on a decision quickly. Then, follow through on that promise.

Step 9: Make the Offer. If you have followed the first eight steps successfully, have identified the right candidate, and have effectively sold the firm, it is now time to make the offer. That's right, don't wait. Remember, Millennials are accustomed to instant responses so give them one. They will be impressed, especially when compared to the amount of time other companies make them wait.

This simple step will communicate to the candidate your firm is decisive, knows what it wants, quickly recognizes the value the candidate can bring to the team, and is not bogged down in red tape.

When the day is over, the person who will be their boss, accompanied by the team leader and CEO, if available, should congratulate them and put an offer letter in hand. In one firm, the CEO actually drives to the candidate's house on the way home from work, knocks on the door, and presents the offer letter in person. What a powerful message he is communicating.

IS YOUR WEBSITE AN ASSET OR LIABILITY?

We love to market our team members. Our staff is our real strength. We've all used this cliché because it's true! However, sometimes we inadvertently market them to the wrong people. Figure 6-3 shows the results of one A/E firms six month study on who hits their website. The findings reveal it is not the people we traditional think of-- our clients! In reality, almost twice as many people come to our firm's web sites by accident.

So who does use our web site? The three biggest groups-- competitors, future employees, and headhunters-- may surprise you. Competitors often use our web site to figure out ways to accentuate our weaknesses when competing for projects. Future employees visit to get an understanding of why they may or may not want to work for our firm. Headhunters, that's right. Headhunters visit our site for a very insidious reason. Why? They are looking for talent to sell to their clients!

We all work really hard on staff development. We recruit at colleges, then spend thousands on training, both internal and external. We place advertisements in newspapers and trade journals. We contact people we've worked with in the past and ask them to consider employment at our companies. We even hire headhunters to do our dirty work.

So we aren't happy when a headhunter or a competitor contacts our employees or we lose a good employee— someone in whom we've invested countless hours and dollars.

The last thing we want to do is make it easy for our staff to be recruited. So what do we do? We list our people on our web site, along with their education, licenses, and project experience. Geez, headhunters must laugh as they look at some of our web sites. We sure make it easy for them. Sometimes, this is even the reason competitors hit our sites. Ever wonder how these headhunters and competitors get the names of our people? We often help them.

So if you happen to be my competitor, I'd appreciate it if you would e-mail me your web address. We're looking for a few good people. You could save us time and money by letting us pre-screen candidates on your web site.

When developing and revising your web site, here's a good rule of thumb: If you don't want your competitors to see it, don't post it. If it will make life easier for a headhunter, don't post it.

When re-developing your website, put the focus on where the benefit really is. Focus on a design that will attract potential star employees, especially Millennials who use the web to do all of their research anyway. In fact, get your Millennials together and ask them to help design the web site in a way that other Millennials will find attractive and one that will correctly communicate the value of working with your firm. Take your web site away from your marketing team and put it in the hands of your human resource team, where its real value can be tapped.

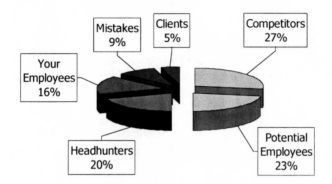

Figure 6-3: Design Firm Web Site Hits

Learning How to Fish

Attracting the best Millennials, choosing them with care and diligence, and keeping them must be as fundamental a part of your practice as turning out drawings or doing site studies. When you take this approach, you not only can create a pipeline through which flow the biggest fish— you can make a bigger fish tank. John McNichol, head of a Philadelphia search firm, suggests five ways for accomplishing this:

1. Build a culture that draws. You want to create a firm for which people would give their eye teeth to work. So you must let people know you are that firm. Build a supportive, empowering culture from the top down, and tell people about it. Believe you are different and then make the difference. Get your staff fired up. Involve them with your vision so they believe it and can convey it. When others hear of it, they will come to you, salmon swimming upstream.

McNichol tells of a friend, president of a 10-office, 300-person engineering firm, who called him for help. "I said, 'Go to each of your offices and empower the people there to look for colleagues from other firms. Give bonuses to people who bring in hires. Get the message out that you are doing something special and going somewhere.'"

2. Make recruiting primary. Fish farms are always being restocked; A/E firms must do the same. "The CEO must see that recruiting is as important as doing the job and making a profit," says McNichol. "Unless you have the people, you can't do the work."

Just as important, make room for different kinds of people. If you meet a recruit who doesn't match your immediate needs but who nevertheless offers valuable skills, think twice before turning him or her away. That person could be your ticket to firm expansion.

"A/E firms are broadening their services," says McNichol. "You must know the needs of your firm but be ready to respond to an individual who might not fit the model." Still, he adds, "You don't settle; you want excellence."

3. Tighten your system. If your recruiting system is haphazard, then so will be the staff you attract. You need to respect the talent out there; they're not waiting for your phone calls. So make your hiring process as rigorous as that of your technical production.

"In this tight market, you must have your act down," says McNichol. "You need people who can make decisions, act within a certain amount of time, and make competitive offers. It takes a system— and it is often handled badly."

He paints horror pictures about people waiting over an hour for interviews, then being met by "turf warriors" who bristle at the sight of new blood— or by an introverted mechanical engineer who never should have been chosen to sell the firm. "It must be done in a managed way," he says. "Senior management must care."

"Caring" also means that your staff knows they have room to grow within the firm, and that when they move up, they will be rewarded for finding a successor. McNichol says. "If you can't bring in your replacement, you are not doing your job."

4. Be true to your pool. If you want to keep your people, treat them as if they matter—because they do. "People who go into A/E often have a great deal of personal loyalty," says McNichol. "But when they see it not coming back, they could get cynical."

He advises clearly communicating what you expect of your team members, but just as important, rewarding them when they come through. "Retention is based on your people having a real sense that if they do their best, they will be recognized."

5. Be true to your school. A/E firms routinely lose the best of the student "catch" because they fail to advertise what a new design recruit wants more than anything: a chance to do great design.

Says McNichol, "The reason people studied design is not to work for a major corporation, but to practice their craft. This is too often not sold."

So go to the universities with this kind of bait— for here is where the fish swim. "I have talked to 600-person firms," McNichol says. "They have never sent anybody to their local colleges, but they need good young talent. So call in your chips. Go to your own schools. Learn who is coming up."

CHAPTER 7

Strategic Training For Millennials

"Organizations that can't-or won't-customize training, career paths, incentives and work responsibilities need a wake-up call."
— Carolyn A. Martin and Bruce Tulgan,
Managing Generation Y

Our business is about selling the services of people. The better trained our employees are, the better value we can provide to our clients. The better training opportunities they have, the more likely they are to stay with us. We know this to be true. We also preach that we believe training, both in-house and outside training via seminars, classes, and conferences to be an important part of our culture.

This is also important to Millennials. As a generation, they highly value cultures that will provide them both training and mentoring. Millennials parents', the Boomers', motto was you can't trust anyone over 30. Ryan Healy, from Brazen Careerist, said Millennials' motto is, "Get as many people over 30 in your corner as you can. Learn from them. And do it better."

What a great opportunity for us as managers and mentors. If we can make training an integral part of our culture, we will both attract motivated Millennials and provide them the tools they need to quickly become producers in our organization. In addition, they will most likely want to stay with the organization because of continued training and mentoring opportunities.

Yet training is expensive and takes away from billable hours. Also the return on our investment is hard to measure. So, although we preach a belief in promoting training for our employees, our follow-through is often weak.

In his book *Practice What You Preach*, former Harvard Business School Professor David Maister presented the results of an empirical study of factors that drive profitability in a professional service firm. His findings suggest firms whose actions matched their spoken vision consistently outperformed firms whose manager's did not 'practice what they preached.'

In the nine primary issues studied, ranging from quality to fair compensation, no issue ranked lower in terms of aligning our "walk" with our "talk" than in the area of training and development. Although training is preached, follow-through is poor.

Now, let's digest those findings for a minute. First, training and mentoring are highly valued by Millennials. Second, firms that deliver to employees what they say they are going to deliver outperform firms that do not. Third, of all the areas firms in the professional service business can 'practice what they preach,' training is the area where they fail the most, at least according to our employees.

Herein lies the opportunity, as well as the reason I am devoting an entire chapter in a book about Millennials to the subject of 'training.' If we can create a culture that consistently delivers effective training and mentoring to our young people, we will easily differentiate ourselves from our competition. We can't just preach it, however. We must deliver in order to reap the true benefit.

A couple of years ago, one of my key Generation X team leaders found himself in a real dilemma. He had a good-sized team of people to keep utilized, but the majority of his team was inexperienced Millennials, most of which were recent graduates. He quickly found the gap between his experience and that of most of his team members was preventing him for being able to delegate effectively. It was the old *catch-22*...he needed to train his people, but he was too busy to do so.

Give 10 Minute On-the-Spot Training

Today, we are passing on more responsibility sooner to our younger, less-experienced project managers, project engineers, and project architects than did the previous generation.

It's great for those with initiative, but more and more, we hear from the non-licensed personnel that what they crave most is on-the-spot training.

Look at it through the eyes of a younger employee. You don't have seniority, you're a team player, and you're constantly pulled on and off projects, doing small segments of work, often without seeing the final results of your efforts.

Employees suggest that what they need is a 10-minute customized training:

1. Provide a brief overview of the project, its objectives, and how their work fits into the big picture.
2. Then spell out the work expectation and what you want accomplished.
3. Finally, and most important for interns and non-licensed staff, give the employees some ways to think about the problem and issues. They are the ones who deliver the product and service to the end-user, your client.

Your project managers need a few hours of non-billable time each week to develop their employees. The payoff may be a well-trained and satisfied future workforce.

Wisely, however, he realized he had only one reasonable option: Bite the bullet and get his team trained as soon as possible. He began an in-house university for his team and hosted lunchtime training sessions twice a month, some led by him, some by others in our firm, and some led by outside vendors. In addition, he tracked down some excellent outside training opportunities and sent his people to them.

It took about six months before he could start to see the benefits. After a year, however, the benefits were significant. As a direct result of his training investment in his team, they have continued to grow successfully, have expanded their reach, and are getting rave reviews from clients, both internal and external. Training is a long-term investment, and as with any such investment, you are feeling pain now with your eyes on the hope of a future reward. If you don't buy the seed, plow the field, and plant the crops, don't expect a harvest.

> *Training is a long-term investment.*

TRAINING STRATEGIES

There are many different types of training opportunities: in-house training, external training, on the job training, and mentoring.

There are varying costs with each of these training methods, so let's focus on methods of maximizing your training return on investment.

Maximizing your in-house training return on investment. In-house professional development programs are grabbing attention in firms of every size. Partially fueled by need for CEUs, better skilled staff, and as enticement for attracting and retaining employees, they are referred to as training centers or in-house universities or lunch-and-learns, or retreats, or breakfast seminars, or whatever.

In-house training is good company policy, vital for employee growth, and unfortunately is falling into dull routines. Joanne Linowes, with executive training firm Linowes Executive Development International, has identified the three big 'nots' for stronger in-house professional development programs as follows:

Ensuring Quality With Younger Team Members

The faster your less experienced staff learn, the smarter they become, the better off you will be.

Everybody learned what he or she knows someplace, usually from other individuals, teachers, colleagues, teammates, etc. It is no different in design practice. Most first jobs are confusing and terrifying for first-timers. They don't really know what they are doing; and if they do think they know, they are probably doing it wrong. Wisdom sets in when we are smart enough to ask dumb questions.

One of the basic mistakes that project managers consistently make is to assume that their staff members know what they are doing. In most offices there are usually a few "gurus" hidden in the woodwork who will take younger staff under their wing and teach them the tricks. But most gurus like to be asked.

* **Tackle training and quality with several techniques.** First and easiest, hold frequent brown-bag lunch seminars. Arrange in-house seminars with your own topics, and require a sign-up sheet to track the progress of those attending.
* **When staffing a job, team up experienced with less experienced staff, often side-by-side.** This has mutual benefits, as the younger staff is often more CAD-literate than the older staff.
* **Finally, adhere to the MBWA (management by walking around) approach to staff development.**

Bottom line: The faster your less experienced staff learn, the smarter they become, the better off you will be.

---

1. Training Does 'Not' Market Itself. If you offer it, will they come? Just because your program has great offerings, does not mean that people will take the time and energy to sign up and attend! And, if staff is directed to take certain courses by their supervisor or HR, that does not ensure they will participate with the requisite level of interest and commitment.

When you have excellent courses and seminars delivered by recognized experts from both within and outside the firm, get your marketing machine in gear! Take some graphics time and skill to make the offerings catalogue and flyers (online or hard-copy) look "exciting." Prepare motivational and enthusiastic course descriptions. Use promotional language and explanations that articulate value-added aspects of each course. When you give the information, descriptions, and registrations process a little flair, the "buzz" reverberates throughout the firm. Grab a marketing moment internally— enhance the entire training effort; ignite interest several times a year.

2. More is 'Not' Better. The most common area for strengthening in-house training programs is to acknowledge that more courses do not necessarily equate to a better program. Offering too much all the time simply dilutes the perceived value of the courses, reducing registrations/enrollments, and diminishing level of commitment on the part of participants.

While it is important to offer a wide range of topics that reflect the breadth-and-depth of your firm's activities and services, the more effective training programs limit the number and courses available within a specific timeframe. If you have, say, 50 possible topics from technical to management to administrative, offer only a small percentage each quarter. Each topic appears to be given special attention. The fewer you offer, the more important each is perceived to be, the more precise can be the outcomes, the more targeted the follow-up.

3. In-House Experts May 'Not' Be Great Classroom Instructors. It is important to have as instructors your principals and in-house experts in management, IT, HR, technical, scientific, design, and construction disciplines. They have the content, experience, and savvy that needs to be shared with others in your firm.

BUT, that does not make them great at presenting their ideas effectively, cultivating a dynamic learning environment, or developing an engaging learning experience.

> **Knowing how to do something does not guarantee the information can be taught in a way that builds skills in someone else.**

A needed topic becomes a deadly seminar if the person serving as instructor is ineffective, dry, or unaware of how to turn expertise into an educational session. *PowerPoint* does not magically turn a person into a good presenter. Knowing how to do something does not guarantee the information can be taught in a way that builds skills in someone else. If the instruction is not effective, the course or seminar is not maximizing time, dollars, or motivated energy.

You will find it very valuable to bring in an outside training consultant to conduct train-the-trainer sessions to provide guidance and techniques vital to helping in-house experts become educators. In addition, for some subject material, such as project management training, bringing in an outside 'expert' is preferable. Someone from the outside comes off as an 'expert' and is often better received than an internal presenter, even when they are delivering the exact same message.

Great training programs produce a skilled and motivated workforce within your firm. Undo the three knots so your firm will provide the highest caliber professional development program!

Case Study
Ready Engineering – A Training Culture

PSMJ Circle of Excellence Firm Ready Engineering is a 27-person electrical and controls consulting engineering firm based in Spruce Grove, Alberta, Canada. Firm president, Lee Ready, shares the following about his firm's culture:

Staffing For Project Needs

Most of the time, Ready Engineering plans for projects just three weeks to three months ahead of time. For some firms, this would create a big staffing headache, but Ready is able to use this scheduling scenario to their advantage. The firm hires casual employees when necessary to meet project needs so they are not sitting on overhead when there is less work available. They have had good luck with converting casual employees to full time. According to Lee Ready, "about 90% of our casual employees work out so well that we take them on full time."

What happens when the work slows down? Depending on the strengths of the people, they are diverted to business development work, internal projects, or research and development. Most of the casual employees are people right out of university or with just a few years of experience. Ready makes it a point to invest heavily in training them so they can make themselves more marketable as soon as possible. "We view staff training as a partnership," explains Lee Ready. "The firm puts up the training dollars but the casual employees are expected to learn on their own time."

The strategy with full-time employees is a little different but follows the same philosophy— people train on the firm's time and their own time but those who train on their own time get increased training budgets.

How does Ready guard against becoming a training ground for competing firms? They have created a small-firm atmosphere and culture and ensure that their employees are well-compensated. They are also careful not to exploit their staff— overtime is rewarded with additional pay or time off in lieu.

Aggressive Scope Management

Ready experiences very few project write-offs, which contributes to their overall superior project performance. During contract negotiations, the firm is picky on scope, but aggressively manages scope during the course of the project. "Many of our clients are not sure what they need when they bring us in," explains Lee Ready. "We recognize that and build enough slack in our project scopes to do what's right on the project. This is the value proposition we offer."

When does the firm allow write-offs? When they don't think they have delivered the value that the client deserves. "I can count the number of times this has happened on one hand," says Lee Ready.

THE ATMOSPHERE EFFECT

Since the right atmosphere affects attitude and attitude affects learning, designers of successful training programs strive to create the most suitable "atmosphere effect."

In-house training programs are the lifeblood for keeping your firm competitive and your staff invigorated. Promoted and delivered appropriately, courses and seminars spur enthusiasm and create momentum for the whole training endeavor. The success of the training program results from several vital factors, including: courses composed of pertinent and easily applied content, motivational and effective instructors, and the "right" atmosphere. Since atmosphere affects attitude and attitude affects learning, designers of successful training programs strive to create the most suitable "atmosphere effect."

The three most frequent mistakes in designing sessions for learning have one thing in common-- they skim over the impact of atmosphere. To fortify your training program, avoid these mistakes:

1. Just "The End." When the course or seminar is over, the participants go back to their daily routine, hopefully bringing with them the new skills and perspectives provided in the sessions. Usually "the end" consists only of a course evaluation. So, the class is over and each participant gives feedback to the instructor or HR department. That helps those who manage the training.

And, beyond the new skills, wouldn't it be nice if each participant leaves feeling accomplished? Consider creating an atmosphere of "Gee, this was really worth the effort." It is important to take the time to recognize their participation, acknowledge their achievement, and make them feel noticed. Invite a principal or department head to give closing remarks. Award each person who completes training with more than an "Atta boy" handshake: Mark their level of effort with something tangible—a certificate or a letter of recognition, etc. This is beyond getting the paper listing the CEUs. When the educational experience is completed, turn "just the end" into a pride-building acknowledgment.

2. Sit Anywhere. The way the room is arranged absolutely affects both learning and attitude. Provide appropriate furniture for the way the information will be delivered. Straight "classroom-style" works best sometimes. Theater-style works best less often than we want to admit. Even if your instruction takes place on a screen, you are not locked into a predictable, boring seating arrangement. Part of course preparation includes evaluating the space to determine where and how people will sit. You can readily create different configurations to encourage a more motivating atmosphere, more attentive behavior, easier interactions. Experiment with circular seating, horseshoe-shaped seating, small groupings, angled rows, and the like. New ideas for seating encourage positive attitudes towards the instructional time block.

3. The session consists of those who sign up. Grouping participants properly is a sophisticated skill. There are no right answers here, but the wrong answer is to just let the course or seminar populate randomly. You need to assess the value of grouping people by job level, job type, department, interest area, etc.

The answers to the following questions depend upon your corporate culture, your firm's training goals, your hidden agendas for the training program, and the intended response:

* Do we group all project managers together?
* Do we mix experienced and inexperienced people in the same group?
* Do we put principals in with other levels or isolate principals in their own training seminars?
* Do we mix departments to encourage intra-firm sharing?
* Is it beneficial to put all Millennial employees together?
* Do we mix new hires with longtime personnel regardless of age?

The composition of the group in each class session affects the atmosphere in the class—the levels of interaction, comfort, learning, and sharing. The properly composed group maximizes the impact of training effort. Create a motivational and encouraging atmosphere and you are spending your training dollars wisely!

PROFESSIONAL DEVELOPMENT PROGRAMS AND THE SECRET INGREDIENTS

When you conduct a training program in-house, you expect to see results—sharper skills, better communication, more technical competence, more successful management and administration. The great misconception, however, is that by simply offering courses and having staff participate, results will be what you are expecting. To make change happen, to make learning "stick," to make the new skills even more valuable to your firm, your training program needs well-constructed courses/seminars that go beyond standard subject matter.

Behind-the-scenes of putting together courses and seminars is the corporate desire to provide a training program that is worth the investment and proves as maximum value to both the firm and the individuals. Good skill-building courses need to be enhanced by being sprinkled with the secret ingredients. Keep the corporate overview in mind as you add:

Ingredient # 1: Attention-Grasp. Grasping attention of adult learners doesn't just happen because they need the particular information. Regardless of how valuable the course participants find the subject matter, regardless of the need to bring certain skill-sets up-to-speed, you know it is a finely honed art to provide quality, results-driven professional development experiences.

Your Millennials are busy with billable activities. When they take time to participate in training courses, seminars, lunch-and-learns, etc., the sessions must grab and hold attention, deliver information succinctly, and maximize use of time.

The secret ingredient that moves a class from "just fine" to "really terrific" is the inclusion of adult-learner-techniques. Training consultants advise that course construction integrate techniques to enliven subject matter so it "sticks." Noticed only subliminally by course participants, these techniques focus on strategies and motives for how adults learn.

Adults, like kids, learn best when information is delivered in a format that makes it easy to acquire the new skills. This varies as each of us absorbs information differently. Some people absorb information best when it is delivered visually. Some listen best. Some prefer to get their information through tactile approaches like models, manipulatives, and props. Still others prefer experiences like role plays and practice problem-solving.

Various lecture styles impact how adults best grasp concepts and facts. Some learn best via storytelling, some by lists of details to memorize, some by analysis.

Areas to note include: arrangement of the classroom, blend of mixed media and mixed instructional styles, varied use of time, repetition of key skills in differing formats.

The secret ingredient for terrific seminars and classes is to engage every type of learner. Going forward, design classes and seminars that build in multiple opportunities and are able to grasp attention and reinforce new learning.

Ingredient #2: Business Development Focus. You can admit it! One key underlying motive of your in-house professional development or continuing education program is to enhance business development. Every course, and any course, can help contribute to bringing in business, just by adding a few key promotional elements.

Consider that tomorrow's successful firms need to build a corporate culture that encourages business development at every staff level, including Millennials. Therefore, your personnel need to be armed with motivating concepts and practical techniques they can comfortably, easily, sincerely, and proudly use to help grow the firm. This includes ways to weave business development into daily interactions and routine meetings.

These are not generic techniques—they should be crafted with the expertise of marketing, training, and business development consultants to reflect your firm's strategies for success and bringing in new work. All this, of course, must be subtly and expertly intertwined within the "regular" subject matter of the course—even those on technical, design, HR, administrative, IT, and scientific topics. Make sure your seminars/classes incorporate your broader agenda for business development. Use these two secret ingredients, not the regular fare.

When you take the extra effort to strategically and professionally add them to your training events, when you allow your larger vision to introduce new approaches that go beyond simply offering a range of courses to fill skill gaps, the yield is effective, well-received skill-building that contributes to employee satisfaction and business growth.

DON'T FORGET THE BIG PICTURE

Allow professional development to include the firm's broader ideas so design professionals at the Millennial level develop an even greater commitment to helping the firm build its reputation and achieve its growth goals.

Your firm's in-house training program can be very effective in providing courses in technical topics, human resources information, presentations, and IT software— personnel will be trained and the professional development program will be evaluated as being successful.

Building skills is, of course, the essential reason to run an in-house training program. Excellent professional development efforts not only provide required CEUs, but also keep your personnel up-to-speed, sharpen their problem-solving and decision-making expertise, and provide an important perk for attracting and retaining Millennials who deliver excellent client service. So, what's missing?

Take advantage of the time Millennials spend in a structured learning setting and focus on how training can deliver something else. Firms that want to maximize the contribution that each employee can make to the growth of the company, need to view training with a broader agenda. Each course you conduct, each lunch-and-learn you offer, each seminar you present allows an often-overlooked opportunity-- the forum for promoting your firm's vision and corporate culture. The best in-house training programs blend big-picture thinking with practical applications.

> *The best in-house training programs blend big-picture thinking with practical applications.*

The big-picture includes infusing staff with the corporate culture—subtly. Maintaining and promoting the vision means planning courses and seminars that dovetail directly with the firm's business plans. When you assess needs and set quality standards, match your decisions with your vision for the firm in the next five years, not for the next big job. Integrate the vision into all instructional sessions— weaving in messages that reinforce the firm's mission, greater goals, and philosophy.

The key to spreading the vision message is to educate all in-house instructors in how to integrate corporate culture into their technical, HR, marketing, and IT subject matter. Formal train-the-trainer seminars work, as well as informal discussions among principals, senior managers, and instructors. Provide a forum for discussing ways to incorporate the global objectives and growth-thinking into ongoing continuing education efforts.

Expand your training goals. Allow professional development to include the firm's broader ideas so design professionals at every level develop an even greater commitment to helping the firm build its reputation and achieve its growth goals.

MAXIMIZE YOUR EXTERNAL TRAINING RETURN ON INVESTMENT

While internal training is great, all training needs cannot be economically delivered in-house, especially in smaller firms. There is a wealth of outside training opportunities available to fill the gaps. So how can you maximize the return on your firm's investment in outside training? I believe the best way is to focus on increasing the amount of positive change that occurs as a result of training instead of focusing on reducing the cost of training.

The student becomes the teacher. One strategy is to require people who participate in outside training to teach what they learn in-house. Although this provides some benefit to your employees who did not attend the training, the greater benefits are as follows:

1. You don't really know a subject until you can teach it. Requiring outside training participants to teach what they learn will encourage them to pay more attention during training. Actually teaching the information will require them to really absorb the material.

2. Leading a training session will improve your team's public speaking and mentoring skills.

3. The act of teaching in a condensed method will require them to choose what parts of the material has the most value to your organization.

4. The teaching requirement will tend to reduce requests for frivolous training.

5. Teaching peers about what you learned in training also provides a built-in accountability mechanism, which I believe is the best benefit. For instance, if someone learns about preparing monthly project reports for each client from a training session, he will be more likely to continue following through with the reports himself in the future, because his peers are watching.

Another beneficial strategy is to send employees in groups of two or more to the same training session. This not only helps build relationships among your team members, but also increases accountability during and after training, promotes the sharing of ideas, and provides a team to work together in the presentation of material learned. In addition, this strategy is especially effective with Millennials who prefer collaboration and teamwork.

Our firm implemented this approach recently and has seen great results. We sent a team of three to PSMJ's *Project Management Bootcamp*. They returned excited about the wealth of information provided and new tools described. Normally, the excitement could be expected to wane in a short period as they again became focused on meeting project deadlines. However, they developed and executed a plan to break the key points from the material presented into three separate lunchtime seminars held every other month.

As a result, they continued to ruminate on the material provided, and had time to practice first what they were going to preach. It made a difference when they could not only teach about sending monthly project reports to clients, but also describe the positive feedback they had already received from clients as a result.

While it does take some extra time and effort, I'm confident you will find the benefits of this approach are well worth the costs, as we have.

MAXIMIZING YOUR MENTORING RETURN ON INVESTMENT

Mentoring has long been a part of professional training. Apprentice programs go back to the Middle Ages. Today, however, mentoring programs are normally done haphazardly, if at all, in professional design firms. Even so, Millennials very much want to be mentored. So, formalize the process. Find likely candidates to provide mentoring, give them a plan for mentoring, and hold them accountable for the results.

Just as a mentor can be an asset to an A/E professional's career, getting hooked up with the wrong mentor can be disastrous. Therefore, you must be strategic when selecting mentors. Here are the elements that can make the mentoring relationship a success or a failure.

The successful mentor should:

1. Understand the importance of mentoring. As a mentor, you must be comfortable with the role and understand the impact that your guidance can have. As with anything, for the role to have value, the importance of mentoring must be both preached and practiced from the top of the organization. In addition, part of the mentor's profit-sharing compensation should be based on their success as a mentor. To determine this level of success, have the young people evaluate their mentors abilities and efforts in this area each year. Remember, what gets measured gets managed.

2. Have similar career paths and interests. Much like a friendship, the mentoring relationship is built on common interests. The mentor's role is that of one who "has been there before" and can dispense advice. This not only applies to technical roles. If a young engineer shows a unique aptitude for business development, find a mentor that can help them hone their talents in this area.

There's an excellent book one of my Gen Xers gave to everyone on our team entitled *Now, Discover Your Strengths* by Marcus Buckingham and Donald Clifton that includes a wonderful test to help identify your strengths. The idea is to find the areas you are naturally gifted and focus on improving these talents and working in roles where they can be used. By using this tool, you can identify mentors and students who share similar strengths and can thus help encourage the best utilization of gifting.

3. Show characteristics of honesty and integrity. Successful mentoring requires mutual respect. As a role model, you must be trustworthy, honest, and worthy of respect. It is important the mentors selected for your firm's program have successfully demonstrated these aspects over time.

4. Openly share knowledge, experience, and advice. There is no room for professional jealousy or unwarranted competition in the mentoring relationship. A mentor must understand the concept that "If you can't be replaced, you can't be promoted." To do so, they must be secure in who they are and in their career.

5. Lead by example as well as by words. It's not enough to be a good communicator. You must lead by example. This adds credibility to shared experiences and advice. Make sure your mentors are those who 'walk the talk' and 'practice what they preach.'

6. Be a respected professional. The mentor should be at an admirable point in his/her career. In fact, the best mentors for Millennials are not Gen Xers, but Boomers. Why? Two reasons. First, there are similarities between how Millennials think and how Boomers thought when they were at the same age in life. However, Boomers have to tap into these memories for them to be beneficial. Second, most Boomers have Millennials for children and this gives them a further understanding of what is going on in Millennial culture.

Millennials should also possess certain attributes for a successful mentoring relationship. The Millennial should:

1. Show appreciation and understanding. Good guidance and advice is not easy to come by. Millennials need to appreciate the value of the mentoring program. In addition, they need to learn to be receptive to constructive criticism. I use the word 'learn' in this sense because often they have never experienced receiving constructive criticism. In the 'promote high self-esteem' culture they grew up in, criticism was often avoided like the plague. This is unfortunate, because everyone has blind spots they must learn to recognize and address.

Top 10 Time Wasters

In order to find time to train and mentor, you must first get rid of other activities that are wasting this valuable and scarce resource. Here are 10 to focus on:

1. Attempting Too Much
Solution: Ask yourself what you are trying to prove. Be realistic. Keep perspective. Stop killing yourself. Stay uninvolved if others can handle it. Stop saying yes just because you want to be appreciated.

2. Confused Responsibility or Authority
Solution: Prepare a list of responsibilities for approval. Identify areas where jobs overlap. Insist on a level of authority parallel to your level of responsibility.

3. Drop-in Visitors
Solution: Recognize that "open door" does not mean physically open, but open to those who need assistance. Meet others outside your office. Stand up when someone enters and keep standing.

4. Inability to Say No
Solution: Refuse to spread yourself too thin. Concentrate your efforts. Count to 10 before saying yes. When saying no, give reasons, suggest alternatives. Say no by showing a list of agreed-upon priorities.

5. Inadequate Planning
Solution: Recognize that every hour in effective planning saves four in execution and gets better results. Recognize that most managers tend to waste time in the same ways every day. Recognize that no memory is infallible.

6. Ineffective Delegation
Solution: Lower standards to what is acceptable, not to your own level of performance. Avoid perfectionism. Relax. Emphasize goal achievement, not methods. Measure results, not activities. Remember that the job of manager is managing, not doing. We'll explore this more in the next chapter.

7. Meetings
Solution: Don't meet without a purpose or an agenda. Only those needed should attend. Test the need for regular meetings. Occasionally eliminate a meeting and see what happens. Or cut time in half for meetings that last a long time. Summarize conclusions to ensure agreement.

---

8. Paperwork
Solution: Read it once and handle it. Eighty percent of daily intake can be disposed of on first handling. Don't hoard it. Answer on the original when a copy is not essential. Standardize forms, file selectively, and alphabetically control your record retention.

9. Procrastination
Solution: Stop the tendency to allow a crisis to develop so you can assume the role of hero in solving it. Get the most vital task done first. Give the more difficult tasks higher priority.

10. Telephone Interruptions
Solution: Develop a plan to screen, delegate, and consolidate. Set hours for taking calls. Set a time limit. ("Yes, I can talk for a few minutes") Foreshadow ending. ("Jim, before we hang up...") Be candid. ("Sorry, got to go now"). Refer calls to delegates. Plan calls, and list points to be discussed.

---

2. Have career goals like those of the mentor. The person should set career milestones similar to those of the mentor. Ask your Millennials where it is they want to go with their career and then connect them with professionals who have walked this path. Often, Millennials will get a better idea of where they want to go by observing the career paths of your firm's mentors.

3. Openly share knowledge. The mentor can also learn when the flow of information is two-way. Millennials have much to offer their mentors, such as how to understand and use technology to its fullest benefit, and a better understanding of what makes Millennials tick. Encourage your mentors to learn from Millennials as well.

4. Recognize dual roles. Just as young professionals look to mentors, others coming up the ranks look to them for guidance and advice. Encourage your Millennial graduates to work with the Millennial co-ops and interns coming behind them. Not only does this give a boost to your intern program, but it provides valuable mentoring and management experience to your recent graduates.

Build Business Development Habits Early

True rainmakers win business by harvesting relationships they have developed over many years. It stands to reason that the sooner your architects and engineers start developing those relationships, the sooner business will come their way. Indeed, those peer relationships with clients establish when both we and our young are often the strongest and most productive years later when both our careers and theirs have advanced.

Here are a few things you can do to get your Millennials started early:

1. Create the Vision: From the moment a newly hired professional starts their on-boarding process, you should set the expectation that she will be expect to develop business later in her career. If you have a week-long orientation process, devote one hour to the subject of business development. That's about the right dosage at this level of employee. Advise your new employee that if she does a few things every week now, developing business will be much easier later.

2. Help Them Start a Contact List: A contact list is the fundamental tool of business development. It is the storehouse of information on your contacts. It provides a record of the growth of your network. Without one, you aren't serious about business development. Every new employee should be encouraged to start a contact list as soon as she joins the firm. You will find that many young, technology-savvy professionals already have one. Give your new employees a quick training session on the contact database your firm uses. Keep it simple. Focus only on the 10 things they need to know to get started.

3. Ask Them to Collect Five Business Cards a Month: They can collect them from clients, subcontractors, colleagues and other people they meet as they work on projects. Suggest that they enter the information from these cards onto their contact lists as soon as they get them. Get them to look for keepers or rising stars, those people who seem destined to do well. With a little luck, they will have 10 of these each year. By the time they have been with the firm five years, they will have 50 and those 50 people will be the foundation of their business development success.

> **4. Insist That They Take a Client to Lunch:** After they have been with the firm for six months, get them in the habit of taking a client to lunch or breakfast once a week. If possible, these invitations should always be tied to a visit to a client site to minimize the time expended. We recommend that you let your employees expense these meals. That way, you can monitor compliance, and, if they start to fall out of the habit, remind them that taking a client to lunch is expected. If the client wants to pick up the tab, recommend that your professional let him, telling him that it is on condition that she pays when they next get together.
>
> **5. Encourage Them to Make Five Relationship Development Calls a Week**: Call and meeting discipline are keys to making rain. Every professional who has been with you for a year should start building that discipline. Insist that they make at least five calls a week to contacts for no other reason than maintaining the relationship. Help them think through reasons for making these calls that will sound plausible to their contacts. These reasons include checkups on client satisfaction after they have lived with the results of your work for a while, information on business or personal issues that might interest the contact, requests for advice or other help, or an invitation to an event being sponsored by your firm.
>
> Get them started early and more of your professionals will become rainmakers. A little attention to the subject now can produce big returns later.

MENTORING: THE EFFECTIVE USE OF ASSISTANT PROJECT MANAGERS

One of the most effective tools in training Millennials is the role of assistant project manager. I have been using this role on our team for a number of years and have found it to be both an invaluable tool for PMs in training and a tremendous help with my time. Here's what the role is and how it works:

1. An unofficial, official position. The selection of the person to serve as assistant PM is key. It needs to be both someone you trust, has demonstrated strong technical abilities, has shown the potential to be a project manager if given the proper training, and who has shown a strong desire to be a PM.

2. NOT an additional person on the team. The idea is not to add another layer to your team. Instead, take someone already serving a key technical role on the team and add this role along with it.

3. Make it official from the start. This is one of the most important steps. Once you have identified who your assistant PM will be, first let them know and explain what is expected of the role. Then, at the kickoff meeting, introduce this person as your assistant PM to everyone on both the design team and the client's team. Explain to everyone that you will be serving as PM, but in case you can't be reached or are not available to attend a meeting, your assistant will be there to keep the project moving forward.

4. Give them PM tasks to perform. Have the assistant perform some of the PM tasks such as:

* **Keeping all meeting minutes.** Review the minutes before they are issued, but let your assistant produce them. This is a great way to teach them how to pick up on all important meeting aspects that should be documented, and teach them how to communicate effectively through writing.

* **Man-hour budgets.** You make strategic decisions on allocation of fee, while others then work out the details. The assistant PM distributes the fee based on your verbal guidelines. Let the assistant and other team members work with accounting staff to "crunch the numbers" for your approval.

* **Schedule.** Based on key milestone dates that you establish, the assistant PM roughs out the overall project schedule. When the schedule needs revising or updating, you can determine the strategy, establish the new milestone dates, and leave the actual task of updating to the assistant project manager.

5. Pinch hits during PM's absence. Allow them to take the lead on meetings you can't attend because of conflicting priorities. Also, encourage the client to call them when you can't be reached. If you select the right person for the assistant PM role, you will quickly find the client will bypass you on most issues and call them first. Why? Because they are easier to reach and have more time to deal with the client's issues promptly. I have also found the client will still call you first on issues they now need your involvement.

6. Allows PM to handle more projects. Wow, how freeing this has been to my schedule. I now can handle three to four critical projects, and still have plenty of time to lead the team, think about strategic direction, and focus on business development. If I have conflicting meetings, it's not a big deal because the assistant PM can lead the meeting without me.

7. Accelerates PM development. Most importantly, you are supercharging your PM training. By serving in the role of assistant PM, they have to think about project management issues along with design issues. They witness some of the bigger-picture politics that greatly impact a project's success or failure. They're learning how to manage a client through the whole process.

8. Lower risk than "sink or swim" *approach*. An A/E firm's typical PM training involves putting them on a project as PM and *hoping* they will survive. The assistant PM role allows them to learn at their own pace in a hands-on, safe environment, and allows you to test out their abilities, as well as be a safety net through the training process.

As a leader of people, you should never go to a design meeting, project meeting, or other activities by yourself. "Isn't it a better use of resources?" you ask. In the short-term, perhaps. In the long-term, however, the benefits of taking them along with you are huge. The time spent in the car or on the plane after the meeting, dissecting what happened and why, and discussing the next steps is invaluable training that will pay big dividends.

So, identify an assistant PM for you next significant project, follow the steps outlined above, and test the results for yourself.

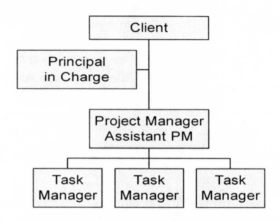

Figure 7-1: Assistant PM Org Chart

CLIENT CHAMPIONS ARE EASIER MADE THAN FOUND

Client champions play a major role in bringing in business. Odds are you have some budding Millennial client champions in your staff and don't even know it.

The role of client champion—one who can relate well to clients and advocate for their interests— requires a specialized skill-set. It behooves firms to foster these skills among their Millennials as much as possible, as successful client champions are invaluable team members: they cement long-lasting client relationships, and they are difficult to find and retain.

Top Five Project Manager Career Roadblocks

These factors are the major reasons many Millennials don't develop into strong PMs:

1. Lack of non-technical skills. Many PMs are promoted from technical positions, and their professional training neglects managerial techniques. Yet finance, communication, leadership, and negotiation are key skills needed to succeed in project management.

2. Too many projects. This prevents you from giving enough attention to each project, especially when management tasks take second place to technical responsibilities on these projects.

3. Lack of authority. Responsibility without accompanying authority leads to frustration. Principals who won't delegate authority for any decisions can damage your effectiveness.

4. Lack of participation during contract negotiations. PMs who don't participate in finalizing the agreement face distinct disadvantages. They miss some of the client's hot buttons that define project success, as well as the subtle give-and-take that takes place during negotiations. Plus they have no buy-in on the project scope and schedule.

5. Lack of knowledge about the client's business. It's simple. If you don't know your client's business environment and individual goals, you can't give them the best project. Learn as much about your clients as possible.

It is critical for your Millennials to begin working on these client relationships early. Often, the clients they have direct contact with are Millennials as well. Their Millennial clients will grow with their organizations and one day hold key decision-making posts. Today, very few people are interested in taking the time to build a relationship with these young clients, so it is relatively easy. Later, when they are promoted to key decision-making positions within their organizations, people will be knocking down their doors and they will become much more resistant to newcomers. Again, it is a long-term investment, but the long-term investments are the ones that really pay off.

People with the right blend of technical ability, experience, and interpersonal skills needed to fill this role are rare in the A/E industry. Because of their scarcity, client champions are best developed in-house. It is easier and cheaper to build your client champions through a strong farm system than by bidding for "high-priced free agents" on the open market. Developing a deep bench of potential client champions should be the goal of every firm.

1. Analyze the competencies needed and assess staff abilities. Which Millennial members have what it takes to become client champions? Make sure you know the strengths of each member of your team, and identify those who are a good match with the needed competencies of a client champion.

For example, the ability to translate technical information into plain language is a key asset. Those who relate well to different types of constituencies—— technical people, tradesmen, planners, and owners—— have client champion potential.

2. Provide opportunities for Millennials to grow and develop. Get Millennials involved with clients early so that they have an opportunity to learn how to relate to them. These interactions will help managers identify those who have client champion potential.

Often, the most difficult qualities for a budding client champion to develop are interpersonal or soft skills. Though the need for some basic inherent aptitude in this area is undeniable, many people can be trained to improve their soft skills. Unfortunately, few A/E firms seem to offer meaningful training in this area. In many cases, new managers are thrown into sink-or-swim client champion positions right off the bat. That's unfair to both the employee and the client. Teach them how to build these relationships.

3. Encourage others client leaders to coach and mentor. If your firm has a manager who excels in the client champion role, you have a natural asset to mentor Millennial client champions. Identify individuals on your team who will benefit by mentoring from a seasoned hand. There is no exact formula for who fits the job description as a mentor. A good client champion can probably relate well to Millennials with high potential. To spur mentoring, make it part of managers' bonus compensation plans, and evaluate their work in this area along with their other duties during performance reviews.

4. Use personal coaches. Personal coaches— outside consultants who offer periodic unbiased advice and informal training— can also help staffers boost their soft skills and client champion ability. Although coaches frequently work on interpersonal skills, they do so on a practical level; their work is not touchy-feely stuff. Advice and guidance tends to be down-to-earth and specific. Find a coach that has experience working with other A/E businesses.

Many firms are offering these one-on-one coaching programs to managers as an added benefit. Because most firms today require principals to provide business leadership— not just technical guidance— employees who aspire to upper management positions value such programs.

Thus, embracing the goal of developing client champions has many benefits. Not only will your firm have qualified Millennials groomed for the role, but you'll also develop a reputation for offering enlightened career advancement training. That can only help both retention and recruiting in the long run.

ADVICE FOR MILLENNIAL PROJECT MANAGERS

There are an increasing number of employees who now report to younger managers who may even come from the Millennial generation. Not surprisingly, age differences can cause real relationship barriers and disrupt team dynamics on a project.

As firms look for the best and brightest leadership, many energetic Millennials are picked as managers.

Here is some advice to share with your Millennial project managers:

1. Remember that you are young and inexperienced. Don't be insulted if some of your direct reports are aware of that, too. Prove yourself without showing off.

2. Get to know each person on your team. Learn what you have to learn from each person. Figure out where each person on the team is coming from and where each one is going.

3. Build an ongoing dialogue with each team member. Talk to every person one-on-one at least once a week, and talk about the work. Gradually discover what you need to talk about (and how you need to talk) with each team member, and develop a good system for keeping notes in a running log.

4. Don't shoot down ideas. Instead, when presented with new ideas, ask for a written proposal with pros and cons, a schedule of goals and deadlines, resource needs, etc.

5. Find at least one wise sage on your team, someone who can tell you the inside scoop, where the resources are, pitfalls, shortcuts, politics, and context.

6. Get results. If your team succeeds, you will gain power and status and rewards for yourself and your team. Then they'll love you, no matter how young you are.

Developing Leadership in Project Managers

Many of the characteristics of a good leader are also necessary for good— and profitable— project management. PMs are, after all, leaders of often very complex teams. To boost the efficiency of your PMs, ask them these questions.

1. Do you solicit information from team members and collect data from all appropriate sources? Are you then ultimately prepared to make a decision and stick with it?

2. Once decisions are made, do you follow through?

3. Do you make realistic commitments, and stick to them? When you say yes, can you be counted on?

4. Do you not only plan your project but also plan your team's and your own activities for efficiency?

5. Do you begin a project or task only after knowing what the final outcome and expectations are?

6. Do you always establish a goal and work to achieve it for each activity?

7. Do you and your team act as if you own the project— and the firm?

8. Do you have stable moods that don't swing widely or erupt into erratic behavior?

9. When referring to you, would your team members say that you were on the side of "overcommunicating" rather than "undercommunicating"?

10. Would you rather effectively delegate authority than complete every task yourself?

11. Do you create an environment in which your team members feel encouraged to excel?

12. Do you learn people's strengths and assign them work that challenges their limitations?

Case Study
Thinking Long-Term-- Finding and Grooming Your Next Leaders

Your first step to ensuring your firm has a next generation of leaders is to be willing, at some point, to turn over leadership. This may take soul searching. After that, you need to come up with a plan for recruiting and developing your next leaders.

But transition in a design firm usually happens like this: owners meet with consultants, attorneys, and accountants and spend months developing a "perfect" buy/sell agreement. They focus on the terms, conditions, and accounting. No thought is given to the next generation; the principals assume that, when the time comes, the chosen group of long-time loyal followers will "be in place" to take over.

This is a dangerous assumption. Good followers don't always make good leaders. But few firms define the traits of their future principals or develop young professionals to take leadership roles. And too many current principals haven't thought enough about giving up that role.

Finding them

Thomas C. Seckman, P.E., chairman emeritus of Nashville's Smith Seckman Reid, Inc., is one principal who did that thinking. Between 1984 and 1994, Seckman, from whose vision his firm had sprung, led his staff through a successful transition in which, right from the start, he planned to relinquish leadership. In the process, the firm grew from 100 people and $5 million of revenue to 365 people and $40 million of revenue.

Says current SSR President and CEO J. Robin Barrick, P.E., "The transition worked well because the founders started early and gave the process 10 to 12 years. They didn't wait until they were 65. Also, they were willing to transition leadership as well as ownership. They were willing to give up control."

From his firm's own successful transition, Tom Seckman shares these 10 pieces of advice for ownership and leadership transition:

1. Have a long-range plan for hiring a specific number of graduating engineers each year.

2. When you interview, involve people in your firm who are experienced interviewers. The higher the level you're hiring for, the more qualified the interviewers should be.

3. Look not only for technical skills, but for people skills as well.

4. If they are willing, give engineers and other selected prospects a personality test. It will help you see how the person will fit the job requirements and the work environment.

5. Hire an outside professional to help in interviewing someone for a key position.

6. Check references.

7. If you're not sure about someone, give yourself time to think about it. If your discomfort doesn't go away, don't hire the person, even if the need is critical.

8. If you use a recruiter, don't count on him or her to screen prospects.

9. The best contacts come from referrals.

10. Be careful of nepotism. Family members can add a lot to the business, but they can also drive talented people away. Be as objective about their potential and performance as you are about people from the outside.

Grooming them

Once you've recruited talented, ambitious professionals, pay attention to developing their abilities and their leadership potential. Bring them up!

Here's more advice from Tom Seckman:

1. Encourage prospective leaders to broaden their education. If they're likely to have a role in management, an MBA might be a good idea. Help them pay tuition.

2. Attend outside conferences and encourage employees to attend them, too.

3. Delegate as much authority as possible, perhaps even before you think people are ready.

4. Expect people to make mistakes. Don't be judgmental, but help them correct their mistakes and move on.

5. Get your ego out of the way; share the spotlight.

6. Give prospective candidates experience serving on committees within the firm.

7. Give them experience managing a branch.

8. Provide alternate career paths for people not interested in management; you need career engineers, too.

9. Make sure key employees understand you are developing them for potential leadership positions.

In addition, here are some other suggestions for grooming prospective employees:

* Make it clear that everyone in the firm is expected to develop his or her talents
* Write a development plan for any individual you've chosen as a potential successor
* Review each individual each year to check on his or her progress and determine current development needs
* Make sure employees understand the criteria for leadership and ownership
* Make sure prospective leaders understand the distinction between ownership (investment) and employment (doing a good job for pay)
* Train prospective leaders and owners in the business side of running the firm

CHAPTER 8

Empowering Millennials—Delegation 101

"Henry Ford II, as I would learn firsthand, had a nasty habit of getting rid of strong leaders."

— Lee Iacocca

My father grew up on a tobacco farm in rural North Carolina, as did his father and grandfather. Several years ago, my father told me a story about my grandfather's and great uncle's farm management techniques. Grandfather's approach was to direct each of his laborers to work a row, while he would also work his own row. However, my grandfather's brother took a different approach to running his operations: he never worked a row, but focused on watching over each of his laborers on their rows.

Who do you think was the more productive farmer? Being young and full of questions, I asked my father. I was confident the answer was my grandfather. To my surprise, the answer was my father's brother by a wide margin.

FAST FORWARD

Many years later, my wife and I were having dinner with one of my business partners and his spouse. We were discussing the weak operating profit margins his group was experiencing when his wife lamented that her husband had increased his work hours by 10 percent over the past three months but the revenue numbers had barely moved.

Immediately, the memory of the story from my childhood returned. The root of the problem was this partner focused on "working his own row." In this case, he was spending the majority of his time doing design calculations and sketches for CAD technicians. Most of these tasks could be performed just as well by a mid-level, non-degreed designer.

The problem was amplified because this partner oversaw a 30-person production team, which was in desperate need of leadership. No wonder increasing his production time by 10 percent had little effect on revenue. Imagine what effect increasing the entire group's utilization by 5 percent— or the equivalent in efficiency improvements— would have on the bottom line.

MAKING THE TRANSITION

Why is this concept so difficult to grasp in our industry? Like many other professions, the lack of leadership and management training we receive in college leaves us unprepared for this crucial transition. When a call for leadership is issued, we default to what we know. Other professions, such as pharmacy, medicine, and law, are recognizing the need and including business and leadership training within their degree programs. Yet, I don't know of an architectural or engineering program that includes any business management courses. I do, however, know of many partners in our industry who believe business management issues are of little concern and can be addressed properly through common sense. Yet, these same people believe the intricacies of their own disciplines require significant formal training. Go figure.

> *Like many other professions, the lack of leadership and management training we receive in college leaves us unprepared for this crucial transition.*

Management expert Peter Drucker wrote, "The generation and direction of human energies *is* the task of management." As we develop in our careers, our role as managers increases in its ability to affect outcomes of our organization. The reverse is true of our role as "row workers," as personal utilization rates should decrease throughout a career.

There are many actions we can take to increase the efficiency of those specifically involved in production. Some of these actions include:

* Ensuring team members have the proper tools to perform tasks efficiently
* Developing well-thought-out proposals that clearly define the scope for both owner and project team
* Integrating the firm's overall vision and strategy throughout the organization
* Leading in the area of team training
* Focusing on creating a pleasant and enjoyable work environment that will attract performance-driven Millennials

It seems there is often a voice within which screams, "Any task other than pure design is not real work!" As a result, little value is assigned to the very important roles required to effectively manage an organization. While this approach works and is somewhat necessary with a small team, it is not scalable. The autopilot approach to managing a large organization is a recipe for disaster.

Some very talented architects and engineers will not have the desire or skill set necessary to ever develop into a good team leader. This is not a problem as long as they are willing to leave the management issues of the firm in the hands of skilled managers.

It is so tempting to jump "in the row" and revert to "row working" when the heat is on and project deadlines are rapidly approaching. Yet this is the very time when leadership is most required.

You may be the best row worker in history, but if you don't change your thinking as your organization grows, you become the bottleneck.

Does Your Firm Suffer From "Principal Bottleneck"?

Sometimes, the best way to spur growth in your firm means letting go of your work.

If you are struggling to grow and expand your firm, the problem may be staring at you in mirror.

According to a colleague of mine, PSMJ consultant Mike D'Alessandro, it is often the principals that unknowingly stifle the growth of their own firms. "I had a consulting job with for a 40-person firm in the South," D'Alessandro says. "The firm owners wanted to grow, but they had not been able to do so since they started the firm 14 years ago.

"After asking some questions, I soon realized that every action and decision made in the firm went through the five principals. They managed every proposal, project, and client relationship. Therefore, no one else in the firm had any authority, or the chance to develop new skills and responsibilities. It was a classic case of 'principal bottleneck.'" This trap is common among A/E firms. It is hard for many experienced principals to let go of work. But if a firm wants to grow, principals must make it their top priority to grow the project management culture and client relations culture of their firm.

Give your PMs authority. Whether it is proposals, negotiations, or client relations, you need to take a step back and give your project managers more authority with the client and the project. "Once you give a PM authority over certain responsibilities, you cannot circumvent that authority," says D'Alessandro. "Otherwise, you face communication breakdown on the project, and your client loses faith in your project manager.

Check yourself

Follow these seven tactics to keep you from contributing to principal bottleneck:

1. Be mindful of old habits. Particularly during stressful times, it can be comforting to immerse yourself in old, safe activities. Remember, though, these activities are no longer your responsibility.

2. Learn to delegate. Effective delegation allows your company and your employees to grow. It also frees your time to do the things you should be doing in your role as a firm leader. the job won't be done as quickly or as well as you could do it. And you're right. But by not allowing employees the opportunity to fail, they won't learn and will never develop the skills that will make them effective. You will also continue to spend your time in activities that keep you— and your firm— stagnant.

3. Trust your staff. Trust is critical when you're trying to pull people together to do a job, and it goes beyond "lip service." Trust means that you will give them more responsibility along with the accountability that goes with it. You will allow— even expect— them to make mistakes and will understand that they want to do good work.

4. Learn to focus on the big picture. It's your staff's job to worry about the details of getting a job done. They must deliberate over small techniques, devise ways to monitor day-to-day activities, and deal with inherent crises along the way.

5. Know your strengths and weaknesses. As a business owner, you must be aware of your strengths and weaknesses so that others can support you in filling the gaps.

6. Hire the best. The key to successful direction is having good people to direct. So hire the best. Make sure your people have the strengths that you need to move ahead. And support the manager who tells you of personnel who are lacking in certain areas. Provide the training necessary to gain these critical skills.

7. In fact, hire people smarter than you. A common problem for new owners and managers is "protective hiring." You're not confident enough of your own skills to take the risk of hiring a "hot shot" who might someday take your job. Remember, if your employees don't look good, you don't look good. There is no such thing as an overqualified job candidate if he or she wants the position.

EFFECTIVE DELEGATION:
UNLOCKING THE KEYS

"The best executive is the one who has sense enough to pick good men to do what he wants done, and the self-restraint enough to keep from meddling with them while they do it."

— Theodore Roosevelt

If you want a more productive staff, stop designing and start managing! If ever there was one thing holding engineers and architects back from reaching their full career potential, it's the lack of ability to delegate effectively. While traveling the country working with design firm principals, I always preach the same message: "You have two choices in our business, and only two." After a pause to let the anticipation build, I continue, "You can be successful...or you can be in control."

It's always interesting to watch the body language in the audience at this point, because now we have gone from 'preaching' to 'meddling'. The difference between the two? 'Preaching' is when the message applies to the person next to you. 'Meddling' is when it applies to you...and there are few architects and engineers that do not wrestle with the control issue. Why? We're control freaks, of course. Our motto is "If you want it done right...do it yourself." In fact, I believe this character makeup is part of what created the desire within us early on to be an architect or engineer in the first place, and it is part of what makes us good at what we do. It's really part of our strength!

However, every strength has a corresponding weakness, and our desire for 'perfection' leads to an inability to let go of 'control.'

Not only will this stifle your career potential, but it will also stifle and drive away the best Millennials under your care. They don't want to be micromanaged! They hate it!

So, how do we overcome our need for control? Personally, I found it is in replacing our old motto with a new one. Now, before you read it, I recommend you sit down, take a deep breath, and relax…because you are probably not going to like it. My motto is "If someone you are responsible for can do an activity 80% as well as you can, they should be doing it!" Think about that for a moment. You may wonder why 80%. You may think that is not acceptable for the 'quality' you want to deliver.

What I have found is 80% works and here's how: When you identify a task someone can do 80% as well as you, sit down and train them to do it, and then review the results. The first time, it will take you a good bit longer with this method than doing the task yourself. The second time, it will still take a little longer. By the third time, however, if you are working with a motivated and talented Millennial, it will not take as long and your time commitment to the task will drop off exponentially from there.

Interestingly enough, I have found that, by the fourth time, the delegated activity will not only require little to none of your time, but the person doing the task will do it better than you would have in the first place. Why? For one, they are probably closer and more focused on the task as it relates to the project they are working on, but more importantly, they have more time!

However, remember the threshold. If they are not yet capable of reaching the 80% mark on the task, it is not yet time to delegate. Either find someone else to delegate the task or get them the training they need reach the 80% threshold.

So, Millennials want to take on more responsibility and we, as managers, desperately need to free up time from 'urgent' activities so we can have some time to also work on the 'important' activities.

Trying to figure out where to start delegating? If you are a principal, and have Millennial, or young Gen X project managers under you, make sure you are serving the role of a principal and they are serving the role of a PM. Figure 8-1 identifies how principals work with strong project managers. Ask yourself which of the PM roles you currently control and come up with a plan to delegate that activity.

Activities	Project Manager	Principal
Fee Proposals	Prepares	Approves
Fee Negotiations	Participates	Directs
Team Selection	Requests	Approves
Performance Evaluations	Inputs	Performs
Removing Non-Performers	Recommends	Acts
Design/Technical Decisions	Meets Standards	Set Standards
Client Relations	Maintains	Oversees
Future Work	Secures	Approves
Accountability	Maintains	Rewards/Punishes

**Figure 8-1: How Principals Work
With Strong Project Managers**

RECOGNIZE WHERE EXPERIENCE ADDS
THE MOST VALUE

I'm not a very good golfer, but I still end up playing a couple of times a year. It is funny how the game of golf often mimics life. There are many words of wisdom offered by more frequent players to hackers like myself, whether or not you ask for it. One you continually hear is "Drive for show, putt for dough," suggesting the all-important and often-neglected role of the putting game in a golf score.

One day, while playing with my father-in-law, and receiving these words of wisdom once again from our playing companions, he looked at me and said, "You know, there may be some truth to that saying, but I have noticed the rest of the game is a lot easier if I can get my tee shot a fair distance down the middle of the fairway."

Energizing Employees and the Power of "I's"

For powerful tools to develop motivated, energized staff, managers need look no further than their daily interactions with employees. This is the expert view of Bob Nelson, president of Nelson Motivation, Inc., of San Diego, CA (nelson-motivation.com) and author of *Managing for Dummies* as well as *1001 Ways to Reward Employees*. Nelson uses the letter "I" (for Interaction) as a mnemonic device in referring to these tools.

Here are five "I's" he feels are the most powerful:

1. Interesting and important work. Every employee should have great interest in some part of his or her job. As the management theorist Frederick Herzberg once said, "If you want someone to do a good job, give them a good job to do." Yes, some jobs may be inherently boring, but you can delegate to anyone in such a job at least one stimulating task or project.

Name the person to a suggestion committee that meets weekly, or to some other special group. The time away from his or her regular job will likely bring renewed energy and productivity.

2. Information, communication and feedback on performance. With presumed employment for life largely a thing of the past, employees want more than ever to know how they are doing in their jobs and how the company is doing in its business. Start telling them how the company makes money and how it spends money. Make sure there are ample channels of communication to encourage employees to be informed, ask questions, and share information.

At least some of the communication channels should directly involve management in a non-intimidating setting. Soon you'll have them turning out the lights when they're last to leave a room.

3. Involvement in decisions and a sense of ownership. Involving employees, especially in decisions that affect them, is both respectful to them and practical. People who are closest to a problem or a customer typically have the best insight as to how a situation can be improved. They know what works and what does not, but often are never asked for their opinion.

As you involve others, you increase their commitment and ease in implementing any new idea or change.

4. Independence, autonomy, and flexibility. Most employees— especially experienced, top-performing employees— want to be given room to do their job as they best see fit. All employees appreciate having flexibility in their jobs. When you provide these factors to your employees based on desired performance, you increase the likelihood that they will perform as desired— and bring additional initiative, ideas, and energy to the job as well.

5. Opportunity for learning, growth, and responsibility. Everyone appreciates a manager who gives credit where it is due. The chances to share the successes of employees with others throughout your firm are almost limitless. In addition, most employee development is on-the-job development that comes from new learning opportunities and the chance to gain new skills and experience.

Providing new ways to perform, learn, and grow as a form of recognition and thanks is very motivating to most employees.

Behind all of these techniques lie the basic principles of trust, respect, and having the best interests of your employees at heart. You will never get the best effort from employees today by building a fire under them. Rather, you need to find a way to build a fire within them to obtain extraordinary results from ordinary people.

Soon afterwards, I played in a charity event as the high handicapper (the person who shoots the highest score relative to par, with higher scores being worse than lower scores) on the team. In this particular event, everyone played their own ball from the location of the best tee shot on the team (which was never mine). Wow, what a difference it made to my game.

Applying the lesson. Projects in our business are much like playing a hole on a golf course. Some are short with little tolerance for error. Others are much longer, offering more forgiveness for errant shots. These offer more opportunities to beat par for our profit targets.

As in golf, we often step into the project giving little thought to the many obstacles between us and our end goal. We rush to get the project moving forward. We "hope" our team will work out the details during the process. However, "hope" is not a strategy! Unfortunately, by that next shot, we are deep in the woods facing new, unnecessary challenges.

There are many ways we can focus on making that first drive successful, such as:

* Developing a scope of work so well communicated that it can become the project checklist for our production team
* Negotiating a fee that will support the effort required and will meet or exceed profit targets
* Defining the clear project goals by which success will be measured by both owner and your firm
* Identifying the potential pitfalls and incorporate tools in the contract to mitigate or minimize these risks
* Setting internal targets to exceed the requirements for the first phase of the project or, in golf parlance, hit the drive far down the fairway
* Defining "optional additional services" in the contract, so the owner fully understands what is outside of the scope

* Communicating clearly to your team members all of the above

Just like playing a golf hole, clients rarely remember how a project began, yet never forget how they end! Although great recovery shots from the woods are memorable, they are also rare. And while closing out a project, like putting on a fast, undulating green, is an art form of its own, the project that starts well has the greatest chance of finishing well.

Unfortunately, as principals, we do not have the luxury of playing one hole at a time. We have multiple projects in various phases of design, construction, and closeout along with ongoing marketing and management responsibilities. These demands compete with the amount of time and effort required to properly tee the ball up on a new project.

Time-Saving Tip: Get It and Get Rid of It

Senior project manager John Bruszewski, P.E., of the Midwest engineering and architecture firm Bonestroo and Associates, offered a time-saving tip he calls, "Get It and Get Rid of It".

This time-saver applies to anything that crosses your desk that will take less than two minutes to complete and also to anything that can be delegated to another team member. By immediately tackling the small items that can be handled on the spot, you save time by avoiding time-consuming pile-up of letters, e-mails, phone calls, and other paperwork.

"Do not let these accumulate on your to-do pile," says Bruszewski, "as it will take twice as long to complete."

THE PARETO PRINCIPLE

"Mark Twain once remarked that great things can happen when you don't care who gets the credit. But you can take that a step farther. I believe the greatest things happen only when you give others the credit."
– Dr. John Maxwell, *The 21 Irrefutable Laws of Leadership*

Time is a limited resource for everyone. The only difference between you and others is how you choose to spend this resource. As a principal, there are very few investments in our business with a greater long-term return than directing the front end of projects. As such, this task provides an excellent example of where we really can add value to our teams and organization as a whole.

How do you figure out which of the many activities give you the most return? The answer lies in the Pareto Principle. Pareto was an 18th century Italian economist who first recognized a powerful economic relationship. According to Pareto, people, teams, and organizations get 80% of their results from 20% of their activities.

I recently had a conversation about the Pareto Principle with a friend of mine who is a corporate manager for a mid-size engineering firm based on the East Coast. This individual has a gift for data mining, one of those rare professionals who can take mountains of information, wrestle it into submission, and figure out what it is telling you. He had just reviewed his firm's operating numbers over a number of years and came to the following shocking conclusion:

* 80% of the firm's profitability came from 20% of their clients
* 80% of the firm's headaches came from 20% of their clients, although it was a different 20%
* 80% of the firm's profits were generated by 20% of their firm's principals

*   20% of his personal activities lead to 80% of his personal results

For years, I have observed the world through the lens of Pareto's principle and found it has universal application extending to nature, family, non-profit organizations, human resource issues, etc. I have found it to be the secret of getting beyond just doing things efficiently and focusing instead on investing your time where you will get the greatest return. My friend has experimented with the Pareto Principle in his own life and quickly found results. "This stuff really works," he exclaimed, as if a weight he had been carrying for years was finally removed. It's frustrating when you can't see the light at the end of the tunnel and exhilarating when it is in full view.

> *It's frustrating when you can't see the light at the end of the tunnel and exhilarating when it is in full view.*

Here's a personal example of how you can put this principle into practice. A number of years ago, I recognized setting up projects correctly from the beginning was one of the activities within the 20% that lead to 80% of our team's long-term results. After recognizing this fact, I quickly delegated or ignored other activities so I could put my best effort into ensuring every project our team accepted was set up for success. After a while, our team's results improved...dramatically! Because the jobs were well set up, on average, they finished better. Not only were the projects more profitable, there were less headaches along the way and the clients were happier with the end result. This freed up not only my time, but the time of other team members to invest in other places.

I eventually realized, however, applying the Pareto Principle to your schedule is not a one-time event. If you can get your hands off the 80% and focus on the 20%, your results will most certainly improve. Yet, eventually, if you look again at the 20% that is now 100% of your focus, you will again see 20% within these activities resulting in 80% of your results. I call it Pareto's Law of Compounding Returns.

For instance, after getting "good" at setting up projects well, I realized I had three team leaders who could take on this activity. This was necessary as well because as our team had grown; this activity was taking up a considerable amount of my time and keeping me from other activities needed to effectively lead our growing team. Here's how I did it:

Step 1: Communicate Why It Is Important. I began by taking these three team leaders to play golf one day. Somewhere in the round, as one of them walked up to the tee box and prepared to make his shot, I walked up and stepped on his ball, pushing it into the ground as far as I could. Then, I looked at him and said, "Go ahead, fire away." Of course, as you might imagine, he looked at me like I was nuts. As we continued the round that day, we began to discuss how project management was like golf. In addition, we discussed my strategy for moving them into this role of teeing up the ball on their projects.

Step 2: Get Them the Training They Need. The three of them found a PSMJ *Project Management Bootcamp* program they could attend together. The program provided intense training on the project manager's role in setting up projects for success.

Step 3: Show Them How. For the next projects that came through their teams, they took the lead on setting them up. They did the first draft of the proposals. Amazingly, due to the training they had received and their own talents, the proposals included some great elements I had never thought of. Even so, a significant portion of my time was required the first few times.

Step 4: Reap the Harvest. Very quickly, my time commitment diminished, the quality of our proposals increased, and their buy-in and understanding of the scope rocketed. Funny how much easier it is for a PM to manage scope creep when they set up the project. I still review all proposals on our team before they go out the door, but now I'm just more of a second set of eyes than anything else. I'm amazed at the quality and detail of these proposals.

The idea is to find the activities within the 80% of your day which can be delegated and the ones that should be ended or ignored. Then focus on the other activities in which you add the most value to the organization. Ensuring a project is set-up correctly is an example of a high-value task that requires experience and today may be in your 20%. As you grow your team and yourself, however, this task may one day move into the 80%. Actually, that's the goal!!!

Stay Sane By Delegating

Question: *I've been placed in charge of training interns and a project architect, but I'm already slammed with multiple projects. How many hours should PMs be putting in a week on training?*

Response: Instead of spending time teaching, train them by passing on some of your work. Delegating is the secret to getting your life back. While you might be able to perform the task faster than the person to whom you delegated it, the team member will become more efficient after practice. In the end, he or she will have learned a new skill, and you will have more time to spend on larger issues.

Follow these steps:

* Give them the available information for the task.
* Ask them what additional information is needed.
* Clearly define what you expect.
* Agree on the proper approach, but don't confuse "different" with "wrong." The person to whom you delegated the task may have a better way to get the job done.
* Agree on a completion date, and level of effort.

If the person who gets the delegated task needs more help, provide 10-minute on-the-spot training. You should also come to grips with the fact that newly introduced tasks will be 30% different and 10% wrong.

STEPS TO BETTER DELEGATION

Delegating means taking responsibility. It means finding a way to complete a project with greater success than if you were to do it yourself. And if success is what you want, you'll need to go the extra mile. That means finding the right people with the right talent resources you know can deliver. The Millennial generation is a great place to find them. Once found, you must leverage those resources. That is your responsibility.

Here are five key components of effective delegation:

1. Go for attitude as much as for aptitude. When you're delegating, you naturally want someone who can do the job. But, equally important, you want someone who can put a fire under the project, especially if the task involves interacting with the team. You not only want the delegate to move on the task, but to get others moving, making them excited and happy to be on the job. You want someone others will heed and like to be around, who generates team spirit, who adds a chemical that raises the team's octane to the next grade.

2. Clearly define the product you expect. Give your delegate a "go-by," a well-drawn example of the product you're after. This will save time. If you want a set of calculations, show your delegate a set from another project that uses the same approach. If you need a project management plan, give your delegate a sample format, something to "go

> *Your delegate knows exactly what you want, you're more likely to get it.*

by." If your delegate knows exactly what you want, you're more likely to get it. And the wheel will not have to be reinvented.

When delegating, we may trust that a person has the skills to understand both a problem and a solution, and we often think it would be insulting to suggest that the person may not understand our point of view.

Unfortunately, this may be misplaced trust, not through a fault of the listener, but through a fundamental fault of our own— we expect the person to know what we mean in the absence of sufficient proactive communication of that meaning. Without clear communication of intent, the team member can only fill in the blanks based on his or her own personal experience.

Caution: With creative tasks, imitation can be the kiss of death. If, for example, you are assigning part of a proposal, you don't want the delegate using boilerplate. You want the "sell" to sound fresh, directed at this specific project.

3. Get immediate feedback. Feedback is essential to effective delegation. Immediate feedback communicates belief of understanding. Consider the following example:

Tom, a project manager, approaches Jim, one of the project team members. He says, "We need a structural framing plan for the West wing by noon next Wednesday for a meeting with the client." He writes down the key points of the communication.

Jim confirms that he understands the order: "You need a framing plan for the West wing by noon next Wednesday. I'm all over it," he replies. The employee leaves with his copy of the written notes.

Jim's immediate feedback to Tom indicates that he understands what needs to be done.

4. Agree on scope, schedule, and budget. When you delegate a task, you want the delegate "looking into your mind." You need crystal-clear mutual understanding of the scope of the delegated job (the "go-by" could be an indicator), of work schedule and deadline, and of the budgeted cost. You and your delegate must agree on these three; if one changes, the others will, too.

5. Set up effective control devices. Once you hand a job to a delegate, don't just walk away! Schedule a series of checkpoints when you both evaluate progress and make needed course corrections. If the job veers off course and you catch it after two days, it will take a lot less rework than if you don't catch it for two weeks or two months.

6. Do not confuse *different* with *wrong*. Delegating means giving the job to someone else. So expect

> *Delegating means giving the job to someone else. So expect that person to do the work differently than you would.*

that person to do the work differently than you would. That's just human nature. Rather than reacting to such difference and assuming it is "wrong" (That's not how I would do it!), try looking for value in that person's difference, value you might not have added yourself.

Being a leader means bringing out the best in your people. So, if your delegate's work is different than yours, try assuming it is "right" or even better. Support his or her best talents. That way, you'll have two sets of best talents: yours, and your delegate's.

7. Monitor progress. Even with proper communication and upfront feedback, a delegated job can go off course without proper monitoring. It is important to schedule periodic progress reports in order to ensure progress towards completion. If the delegatee in the example above is left unmonitored until the due date for the assignment, the supervisor may be surprised by the results.

"I need that framing plan of the West wing now," Tom says on Wednesday on his way to the planned meeting with the client.

"Oh, that," says Jim. "I didn't finish that. I discovered some peripheral details that needed to be addressed. Chuck and I should take care of those first to avoid problems in the long run."

Tom is flabbergasted. He trusted the employee to complete the task on time. Now that time has run out, Tom will be embarrassed in front of the client. He should have made sure Jim was keeping the goal in sight and making timely progress. If the question of peripheral details had come to Tom's attention, they could have dealt with that and still completed the assignment on time.

MANAGEMENT BY ASKING QUESTIONS (MBAQ)

Delegating means assigning someone to do a task but it doesn't mean telling the person how to do it. Instead, ask a series of logical questions leading the person to find his or her own solution. PM means project manager, but it also might mean people manager. Your job as manager is to bring out exemplary talents and performance in your Millennials. So make them think! Invest time in mentoring them, and you will create a team of self-motivated, self-sufficient players who deliver a project better than you could have blueprinted.

Here's how MBAQ works. A few years ago, I had a young engineer that had been on our team since his sophomore year in college. Extremely sharp and talented, he was quickly recognized as an excellent find by all the leaders in our firm. As he grew on our team over the years, I began to notice that, unlike his peers, he continued to come to my office a lot to ask questions. I did not mind that until I realized the questions he was asking were often ones he should know the answer to. In reality he did but was hesitant to move forward on them. My dilemma? How do I get him to become more confident without saying "you should know the answer so stop bugging me," thus stifling his motivation and keeping him from coming to me when the question does need my input?

Take a Deep Breath

If you are constantly running into yourself coming and going, you're probably creating problems instead of avoiding them. If you're a PM with too much to do, step back and stop making hasty decisions about your work.

Consider the following:

* **You don't have to be perfect all the time.** Quality and perfection are two different attributes. Striving for perfection in every detail of a project can waste time and create stress.
* **Quit responding immediately to "urgent" requests.** Tell people they'll simply have to wait. Take five minutes to consider if the request is truly an emergency or a tempest in a teapot.
* **Add a time estimate for daily items to your "to-do" list.** Set priorities each morning— and each evening for the next day. Don't plan more than you can realistically accomplish.
* **Perform fewer individual tasks yourself.** At the beginning of a project, make time to manage team members for results and to delegate more responsibilities.
* **Take time to complete a task right the first time.** Coming back to a partially completed activity, or correcting a mistake, always takes longer and causes frustration.
* **Take time to plan your work with the objectives and the end result in mind.** Think and plan how to achieve the result, not just what tasks you may need to complete.
* **Ask yourself:**
  1. Is the activity truly necessary?
  2. Should I do it now?
  3. Can I schedule it for another time?
  4. Is there someone else who could do it better?

The answer? MBAQ, management by asking questions. I have taught this management practice to a number of principals and it is always fun to watch. Try it yourself in your own firm. Get two principals. Ask one to be a 'Millennial' coming back in from a construction site. Tell your acting Millennial that during his site visit the contractor just identified a design problem, the owner is furious about it and the Millennial believes the owner is going to pursue legal action against the company. Let him use his imagination and creativity from there.

Now, tell your other principal that he is this Millennial's boss. The Millennial is coming back to the office to tell his boss what is happening and get answers. This principal's job is to resolve the issue. However, he has one limitation. He can only talk to the Millennial using questions. No statements, just questions. Then, sit back and have fun. Watch the Millennial character ham up his role and watch the other character squirm trying not to tell him what he should do.

I applied this method with my young engineer. The next time he came to my door with a question, I bit my tongue and only responded with questions. What I found was 9 times out of 10, he got to the right answer himself. What he found was 9 times out of 10, he knew the answer and did not have to waste his valuable time with me. It really works. Try it!

MANAGEMENT BY WALKING AROUND (MBWA)

Get out of your office! Mix with your Millennials. Visit them in their cubicles. Have coffee with them. Schmooze. Chat. Pal around. Let them know you are with them, on their side. In these casual, "water cooler" conversations, you can learn a lot about what goes on in your project and put them on your team.

Five Ways to Keep Tabs on Delegated Work

When it comes to monitoring delegation, I'm a big advocate of MBWA, or "managing by walking around." This is an effective way to check on team members taking on new assignments. However, one drawback of this method is that some managers tend to hover, or they will check on employees every 15 minutes. To better manage your time following up on delegated work, use one of the following methods:

1. Keep a list of delegated work. Look at the list every morning, and decide who to check on and when.

2. Schedule regular meetings to check in with team members.

3. Check in with the team members at milestones in their work. Make sure you space the milestones far enough apart to avoid "hovering."

4. Set time-limit milestones. For instance, have a team member report back to you when the team member has eight hours on his or her timesheet.

5. Create shared electronic files. This allows you to simply open an electronic folder and check the progress of work without bothering anyone.

Your best approach is to use a number of different styles, based on the type of job and the person doing the work.

I am always amazed with principals who only go to lunch with other principals. What a lost opportunity. I once asked one of our firm's old-timers what they liked most about our firm's founder, who is no longer with us. "Quite often, he joined us for lunch in the break-room" was his response. Often, principals ask me how to get their people to open up more and tell them what they think, share input, talk about frustrations. One of the best ways I have seen is to go to lunch with your team. Spend time outside of the office with your Millennials. Show them you are real.

One time, I went to lunch with seven other people on our team, over half of which were Millennials. Nothing formal. It's fun. It helps you keep your finger on the pulse of the team, and helps them relate to you. Try it!

Signs that You're Not Delegating Right Or Not Delegating Enough

Keep close tabs on how you delegate work as well as the success rate of the assignments you pass on. Make sure that you avoid the following delegating mistakes. Never:

* Let two or more individuals be responsible for the same task
* Overly structure the assignment so the individual has no latitude to make decisions
* Redo the assignment yourself. Nothing undermines trust greater than this.
* Forget to thank a team member for quality work

Red Flags

You know you need to improve your delegation skills if:

* You're just too busy. You are under constant pressure, miss personal deadlines or spend a great deal of time on activities that you would not personally pay your charge-out rate for.
* You're often surprised by team members doing things other than what you expected, and job quality is below the standards you expect.
* Productivity is low or dropping and team members seem less efficient and unmotivated.

AVOID "MESSY" DELEGATION

If you're not getting endorsement from those you delegate to, you can expect problems.

Many project managers have a habit of practicing "messy" delegation. This includes delegating by voicemail or leaving a Post-It® with instructions on a team member's desk. The mentality is "I know the person well enough; they can follow my instructions."

The problem with these methods is that you are not getting any endorsement from the delegatee. The person may be out of the office for part of the week or already overloaded with work.

Whenever you delegate work, always give team members the opportunity to say "Yes, I can do the work in this time frame." You don't need to have a meeting to do this; you just need to make sure you receive feedback.

Endorsement over the phone or by e-mail is acceptable, but if an assignment is more complex, you may need to have a face-to-face discussion.

One of my Gen X leaders has figured out an excellent tool to use to manage delegation. Microsoft *Outlook* has a task list feature. I have used it for years to manage my own to do list. He, however, took it to another level. He uses *Outlook* to send tasks, much like e-mail, to his team. When they receive the task, they can accept it, which then adds it to their task list and sends the leader an e-mail when it is completed,

Whenever you delegate work, always give team members the opportunity to say "Yes, I can do the work in this time frame."

or they can decline it with explanation. Although not as good as face-to-face, it is very efficient and highly organized way of task management. He's so good at it that his team members affectionately refer to him as "The Taskmaster."

Principal Vs. Project Manager

In smaller firms, the principals and the project managers are synonymous. Even in larger firms, principals often manage projects. But in situations where the principal is separate from the project manager, the differences between the two positions must be clearly defined.

The Cost of Confusion

Overlapping responsibility and authority can expose your firm to serious problems:

* **Costly duplication of effort.** If decisions do not coincide, team members become confused and clients develop a poor impression of the firm. Tensions between the principal-in-charge and project manager can damage long-term working relationships. They can also undermine the motivation and performance of other team members.
* **Work falling between the cracks.** When there are misunderstandings about who does what, work doesn't get done and quality suffers.

At the beginning of a project, you need to understand and define your level of authority. Find out if there are any changes in your regular responsibilities. For example, the principal may decide to represent the firm at certain project meetings attended by the client—a role you typically hold.

Record exceptions to normally assigned duties in the project file. Note why certain elements of the project won't proceed according to the norm. With specific assignments, it is easier for the firm to review and evaluate performance.

"Project as Restaurant" Analogy

Principals are always tempted to step in and take over. However, their responsibility should not be the nuts-and-bolts of a project, but to build the business. When they delegate to PMs, it should be clear, consistent, and devoid of second-guessing.

Alan Bollinger, P.E., a colleague of mine and a vice president at CH2MHill, likens the relationship between principal and PM to that of employees in a restaurant.

"The principal is like a maitre d'. He greets the guest at the door, but then passes the guest on to the waiter, (i.e., the project manager)," says Bollinger.

"As a client sponsor, the principal's role is to ensure the client is happy and comfortable. He might be involved in getting client feedback or reviewing the proposal, but the project manager should be the key communicator with the client."

CHAPTER 9

Case Studies

In Chapter 3, we reviewed firm cultural traits that Millennials find attractive. Now let's hear from leaders of some very successful firms who weaved a lot of these traits into their cultures. These firms represent most of the various disciplines in our industry, and range in size from as small as four to much larger. Each of which, however, has been recognized as a PSMJ Circle of Excellence Firm because its overall performance is in the top 20% of firms in the A/E industry.

WHR ARCHITECTS, INC.: THE PEOPLE FACTOR

WHR Architects, Inc. (WHR) is an evidence-based architecture, interior design, and consulting firm specializing in healthcare, research, and university facilities and based in Houston and Dallas. Corporate Marketing and Business Development Director Deborah Burge shares the following:

A unique position

When Tropical Storm Allison devastated the Texas Gulf Coast in 1995, WHR was on site immediately to assess and repair the damage to a major hospital, and a long-time client of the firm, in the Texas Medical Center in Houston. WHR put the energy and expertise of the entire firm into returning the 800-bed hospital to operational status— not because it was the most lucrative thing to do, but because of the critical importance of the facility to the city and the medical community. The firm not only did the right thing, they also did it right, which resulted in another major hospital in the severely flooded Texas Medical Center observing WHR's work and hiring them. They remain a client of the firm today.

While WHR's reputation in the healthcare industry continues to grow, the firm is also increasing its percentage of work in the research and higher education fields. The firm's success has enabled WHR to be very selective about the clients it pursues. "We have chosen to work with mission-driven clients." explains Burge. "We live their mission through the value of the facilities we design and the impact those facilities have on our clients' businesses."

A culture of responsiveness

WHR cares deeply what its clients think. Perception surveys reveal that clients consistently express WHR's drive to provide the best client service possible. "Our president, Ken Ross, says our job is to manage the client's experience, not their expectations," remarks Burge. The level of care and attention to detail translates into innovation in project management and execution as well as in design. Such innovation adds value, but not necessarily costs as the firm has a deserved reputation for managing the goals of the client and the project. "We're known as a fiscally responsible design firm. We work with clients to maintain their schedules and budgets. There have been times when we have lost opportunities because we tell the client what they need to hear, not what they want to hear. If the client wants a Cadillac, but only has a budget for a Chevy, we tell them," says Burge. This approach actually improves project performance because the firm is not tying up resources in a project that is destined to fall short of expectations.

"Once we educate the clients on the real costs and schedules associated with their project, they come back to us when they have secured the necessary resources," explains CFO Gailand Smith.

A high level of responsiveness has proved to be a very effective strategy. WHR reports that 90% of its projects are being done for repeat clients. "We've crossed the threshold from vendor of services to trusted advisor," says Burge, "and our people are proud to live that role."

Collaboration is the key to success

WHR is committed to a collaborative process that involves the client and its users, the entire A/E design team and the builder. "We want the client to understand what we're doing and what goes into the design development process so that decisions can be made at the appropriate time and the project is not delayed or incur unnecessary costs," explains Burge. In order to foster its process, WHR will facilitate a visioning session at the initiation of the project to establish a common vocabulary among the firm, the clients, and the client users so everyone speaks the same language throughout the project. The first-hand involvement of the studios also insures communication is consistent among all the project team members.

While the firm is organized into studios, staff revolves in and out of different studios to maximize efficiency. Project management meetings are held at least twice a month to discuss staffing needs and to deal one-on-one with any concerns. By including subconsultants and other important contributors early in the project, WHR ensures that the design solution responds to the client's needs, stays on budget and minimizes future changes and redesigns.

The people factor

In exit interviews, employees leaving the firm most often cite "leaving the people I work with" as the hardest part about taking another job. The firm boasts a rich diversity of age groups, ethnicities, and background— a strength that encourages an informal mentoring process and a lively learning environment.

Recruiting qualified people is a challenge for most firms in a competitive market. "We're looking for qualified individuals with compatible personalities and a work ethic that share our values. We've tried compromising these requirements at times and it never works out," says Smith.

However, that work ethic doesn't mean endless hours at the office. Understanding utilization is key. "We recognize that people have a life outside the office," explains Smith. "The project managers are looking at their bottom lines, but I follow utilization numbers closely to make sure that people are not being consistently overworked and that we still have the staffing to get projects done."

One of the bright spots in recruiting new talent is recent graduates. Until five or six years ago, WHR rarely hired people right out of college, but now they have found a number of outstanding Millennial architects and interior designers who have raised the bar for the entire firm with the implementation of new software and tools. A mutual mentoring program then evolved with the Millennial staff introducing the more experienced staff members to new technology as the more senior staff coach the Millennial staff on the joys and pitfalls of design work in the real world. An added benefit: college graduate hires actively recruit other Millennial architects and designers to the firm.

WHR hired an HR manager to focus on recruiting at the entry, mid, and senior levels. The investment is paying off. Once the HR manager sat down with the studio leaders to understand their needs, she was able to pay closer attention to resumes, work with a recruiter and is now attracting candidates from all over the country.

Levels of satisfaction

Gailand Smith has been with WHR for 13 years and still looks forward to coming to work. He is not alone. "The types of projects we do and the quality of people we do them for create a strong sense of satisfaction," Smith explains.

Another key to satisfaction lies in WHR's refusal to be complacent. With the firm's reputation as an outstanding project performer solidly supported, WHR is actively building a reputation for design. The firm founder, David Watkins, has taken on the role of design director working with young architects and interior designers in the firm to strengthen WHR's design competitiveness.

The learning environment that this effort has generated has created another level of satisfaction. WHR, and Watkins in particular, actively engage the staff in discussions about the importance of design. In the same way that WHR has become a trusted advisor to its clients, WHR's leaders act as trusted advisors to the staff.

WHR faces challenges ahead as it grows in size, yet one thing is clear: they are headed in the right direction.

LAWSON WILLARD ARCHITECTURE: ATTRACT THE MILLENNIALS WITH TRAINING

Lawson Willard Architecture is a four-person full service architecture and planning firm specializing in residential & commercial design based in San Francisco, CA.

In a small firm, even small overhead expenses take on a far greater significance than in a larger firm. Firm Principal Lawson Willard keeps modest office space in a predominantly retail-oriented neighborhood away from the more expensive areas of downtown San Francisco. "We're definitely a workshop environment, no frills," explains Willard. "We prefer to spend money on technology and salaries and benefits for staff."

Willard looks for newly graduated designers to work with the firm. The prospect of being trained quickly and getting responsibility fast is very compelling to Millennial designers— and it gets them working on managing client expectations quickly. "New people get to do design, project management, permitting, and construction administration work very early on," explains Willard. "It puts us in a position to get them billable more often and more rapidly in the process." This strategy is not without its pitfalls— sometimes Millennials stumble but the firm is small enough to be able to make corrections before there are real problems.

Don't clients get a little nervous about having Millennial designers in the critical path on their projects? "There is no question that this can be an issue," says Willard, "but we overcome it by being very open and communicative with our clients. We are constantly asking for client feedback at every phase of the project— we want to know how everyone is doing. We assess strengths and weaknesses at every turn and make adjustments based on what we learn."

Willard believes leveraging technology is extremely important for success in a small firm. "Technology gives us the ability to provide, design, and produce drawings similar to larger firms. With the advent of building information modeling (BIM), small firms will excel in providing useful information to both clients and contractors. This is a value-added service and an additional revenue stream. The BIM process is making us more efficient and we are able to spend more time on design and less time on documentation."

Business Development by Word-of-Mouth

Most of Willard's clients for the firm's residential practice are new clients, and only some of the commercial practice clients have worked with the firm on prior projects. One way that the firm spreads the word is through AIA/San Francisco's Small Firms, Great Projects initiative done in conjunction with *San Francisco* magazine. "We usually get lots of resumes and other interest in the firm after we are mentioned," says Willard.

The firm also has a long list of happy clients and a good base of contractors and interior designers— both residential and commercial— that form an informal network of referrals.

Principal Differentiators

Why do clients want to work with Lawson Willard Architecture in the first place? "As a small firm, we provide attention to detail and the personal touch that clients might not get from a larger firm. We are agile enough to reallocate resources quickly when projects necessitate it," explains Willard.

What does the firm look for in new staff? "We're looking for confident people—folks who can go into the building department of a large city with a plan and get done what needs to get done," says Willard. "We're looking for problem-solvers with strong life skills. We'd rather have someone with strong non-technical skills and fewer technical skills than vice versa. We can teach them design."

Why a Small Firm?

"I started this firm because I wanted to go after a diverse set of projects. In a larger firm, I didn't think I would have the same opportunities to do that," explains Willard. "I wanted to cultivate contacts in many different areas of design and be able to leverage the strengths and competencies of a small group of designers into these efforts. I wanted to concentrate on design as a discipline—not just a specific niche of it."

THOMPSON, VENTULETT, STAINBACK & ASSOCIATES: ATTRACTING MILLENNIALS WITH GREAT PROJECT OPPORTUNITIES

Thompson, Ventulett, Stainback & Associates (TVS) is a 310-person international design firm with more than 38 years of experience in architecture, interior design, and planning. Headquartered in Atlanta, Georgia, TVS also has offices in Chicago and Dubai. Firm Controller David Frazier shares the following:

Since its inception in 1968, TVS has developed strong expertise in designing large, complex projects, particularly convention and exhibition centers. After 9/11, the downtown in the economy caused some design firms to lay off employees or close their doors forever. TVS, on the other hand, approached these challenging times as an opportunity for exploration and growth, particularly in the international marketplace. As a member of Insight Alliance, TVS was able to explore global market opportunities and receive encouragement from member firms related to expanding internationally. These relationships helped guide the firm into a new era where international work is one of its priorities.

After gaining valuable experience in South America, the Caribbean, Bahrain, and Australia, TVS started searching for new significant international opportunities and developed a close relationship with a lighting designer from India who was practicing in Dubai, UAE. Through the relationship, the firm was introduced to key individuals within the Executive Design Bureau in Dubai. This Bureau serves as a principal think tank, incubator and catalyst for visioning development within the Emirates. Within one year of that introduction, TVS opened an office in Dubai, resulting in six or seven large projects and dozens of smaller feasibility and rendering assignments with multiple clients. These projects all have the potential to lead to more advanced work in the Emirates. Such business relationships in Dubai have led the firm to a dramatic increase in growth and revenue for TVS.

"The challenge with our work in Dubai is ensuring we stay diversified," says Frazier. "It would be easy to put all of our eggs in one basket, that being the booming Dubai market, but we know this strategy would not be a smart, long-term decision." Rather, the Dubai experience has helped TVS develop the savvy necessary for working with a culturally diverse client base. In addition to the UAE, the firm is adding clients in other international locations and working with developers who are impressed with TVS' planning and design creativity.

One location where TVS' convention center expertise is in high demand is China. "China presents a completely different set of challenges for our firm," explains Frazier. "In Dubai, our clients want cutting-edge, one-of-a-kind, exuberant imagery. In China, there is a need for a contemplative, modern architecture fitting in harmoniously with the older, more traditional structures." TVS is in a unique experienced position to do this, having overcome the challenges and building restrictions in the District of Columbia to complete the award-winning Washington, D.C. Convention Center.

Diverse projects attract talent

Looking at the development of this TVS business model, one would be surprised to learn that most of these international accomplishments have taken place within a short time frame. This high-speed expansion has helped thrust the company into the forefront, gaining it even more clients, and, more importantly, helping to attract some of the industry's top talent. Working on cutting-edge designs in faraway places is compelling for young architects and established architects hoping to diversify their portfolio.

TVS is now garnering more attention from design schools because, "architects want to design something that leaves a mark on the built environment," says Frazier.

Although the firm's current projects help attract great talent, the company's overall structure and philosophy is also turning heads. TVS has in place a sophisticated intern development program which helps intern-level designers learn a lot about the many facets of the business. The program also helps young architects pass their registration exams earlier. Yet it's the firm's culture that tends to have designers sticking around for longer periods of time. TVS is 100% employee-owned through an employee stock ownership plan, giving everyone a stake in the company. "Only in a firm where people's financial success is tied to the success of the entire firm, and not just their market segment, can people put their personal wants aside and buy into the bold, strategic plans TVS leaders have put in place," explains Frazier.

Diversity— not limited to location

TVS' success can be attributed to more than their international expansion. The firm has also found a logical offshoot from its convention center business, having identified smaller hotel conference centers as a market segment where the firm's expertise can be leveraged very effectively. "Hotels with conference facilities are more popular these days because of their ability to accommodate smaller business meetings in a private setting. In addition, the facilities deliver high occupancy for the hotels to which they are attached," explains Frazier.

The firm has made a strategic effort to build relationships in the hospitality industry and, as a result, has numerous opportunities to design hotel conference centers because of their convention center experience. "Another upshot to this new business venture is the follow-up work," explains Frazier. "Hotels that expand to accommodate larger conferences and more guests also have interior design needs with which we can also help. One relationship leads to the next."

Future Plans

Today, TVS continues to keep its eye on global markets while working on the development of its urban planning business. "Planning is a wonderful business to be a part of because you get an inside track on future developments," says Frazier. "When opportunities come down the line, planners know about them first. You will hopefully already have relationships in place to seize such opportunities. Relationships are the most important thing. Being a great designer is important, but relationships and reputation get you the work."

NATURAL RESOURCE GROUP, INC.: WINNING WITH PEOPLE

Natural Resource Group Inc. (NRG) is a 125-person environmental consulting and public relations firm based in Minneapolis, Minnesota, with five additional offices that specialize in permitting, inspection, and other services for the energy industry. Chief Financial Officer Roger Blomquist shares the following:

A Fateful Decision

After 9/11, the Enron scandal, and recession of the early 2000s, the energy industry flattened out and the fallout hit NRG hard. In spite of that, NRG embarked on a geographic expansion plan. The company felt that, in order to grow, it needed to expand, to give the perception of being a national company. The specific locations were determined by the presence of its clients and potential clients, the location of its competitors, regional demand for energy and the amount of existing and projected infrastructure. In 2003, the firm made the critical decision to accept poor financial performance and not cut staff. The firm reasoned that if it kept its expertise intact, it would be well-positioned to take advantage of new opportunities when the energy industry began to grow again. They also knew that the first few years after the recession would be very busy as the energy industry played catch-up—and they wanted to be well positioned when it happened.

During the slow period in which staff members were underutilized on projects, the firm invested in project management systems, training, and other administrative initiatives so it would be ready to roll out quickly when the work came back.

NRG's patience paid off. The recently signed U.S. Energy Bill is mandating that US ethanol production double, necessitating the building of 100 new ethanol plants. Depletion of North American natural gas reserves has spurred renewed interest in exploration and high energy prices have made extraction from difficult areas more attractive. Plans are underway to build LNG terminals on the U.S. coasts in order to download energy from other countries into the U.S. energy stream. There is also significant interest in extracting energy from oil sands in Canada and in order to do this there will need to be significant investment in infrastructure like pipelines to move the energy. All of this is good news for NRG.

Staffing for Boom Times

NRG, which planned to hire 50 people in 2008, is winning the talent war by recruiting entry-level people without much experience and making the investment in training and mentoring. NRG is hiring for potential and then training staff to do specific jobs. The firm is paying particular attention to keeping principals focused on providing oversight and mentoring to project managers— making sure that they are operating as true principals and not project managers. Project managers are also charged with mentoring team members and helping them take on critical pieces of projects to develop valuable experience.

NRG is staving off competitors from poaching people by offering compensation packages that are at the high end of the scale, providing a superior benefits package, and taking proactive steps to make NRG an enjoyable place to work. NRG feels that rewarding people and providing them with not only career opportunities but the ability to interact in a social setting is integral to building a team-oriented culture, especially with staff spread out over six locations.

Ensuring Sustainable Growth

How is NRG building the firm to last? It is shifting the lion's share of its marketing efforts to maintaining relationships with their current "A-List" of clients rather than seeking out new business. The firm values relationships with sophisticated *Fortune* 500 clients and makes taking care of them a top priority. NRG has no dedicated marketing department, but has a principal-level "marketing director" and all marketing initiatives funnel through him and he sets the business development direction of the firm. NRG also has four of five principals and some senior project managers who are charged with maintaining client relationships. The key is face-to-face meetings. NRG values relationships based on a handshake and looking people in the eye. E-mail and phone calls are no substitute. NRG has deftly positioned itself as an industry leader and a trusted advisor, and clients are willing to pay for the value that the firm brings to the relationship. Even in a cyclical downturn in the client's industry, the core work will always be available to them.

OLSSON ASSOCIATES: LOOKING FOR PASSION

Olsson Associates is a 550-person firm offering services in the fields of civil, structural, water resources, environmental sciences, and transportation engineering based in Lincoln, Nebraska. Chairman and CEO Roger Severin shares the firm's story.

Many 10-Person Firms

A principal factor in Olsson's success is that the firm is structured as dozens of 10-person engineering firms, which has fostered a strong sense of accountability to clients. This particular organizational structure has provided the firm with a fertile environment for organic business growth— rather than through acquisition of smaller firms. These small business units are entrepreneurial in nature and key people within these small groups identify and pursue business opportunities on many small-scales. "Our people are constantly looking for the next business opportunity," says Severin. "Nobody is sitting around waiting to be handed a project." Most firms of Olsson's size fuel growth by working toward a revenue number developed through a long-term strategic planning process. Olsson fuels growth by making the small business units responsible for picking good projects and good clients that want to work with them.

How does Olsson manage growth in this context? "We are uncompromising in our commitment to the values of superior client service and project performance," explains Patty McManus, the firm's president. "The only yellow light affecting continued growth is any falloff in these areas."

Let the Clients Define Service

While Olsson's organizational structure promotes a culture of entrepreneurism, the firm screens prospective new employees based on their attitude and orientation to client service. "Fifteen years ago, we felt we were slipping away from our core commitment to client service," recalls McManus, "so we surveyed our clients to find out how they defined service so that we would be able to attract and keep service-oriented employees. We worked backwards from what our clients told us. We determined how clients defined service and what kinds of people are excellent at delivering these things. We build our firm to be a place where service-oriented people want to work. It's a work in progress."

A distinct advantage of being a large firm made up of many 10-person firms is the ability to adapt and change very quickly. Olsson doesn't have much bureaucracy for a firm of its size so ideas can be implemented in short order and the firm is always evolving. The other factor that contributes to Olsson's agility is it understands that new and different ideas call for a diversity of thought among the staff. "Twenty or 25 years ago, an engineer had to prove technical excellence to be deemed a success in the firm. Today, we also rely on service-oriented people who maybe are not as proficient technically," recalls Severin. "Not everyone can wear every hat. We'd like very much to have even more people for whom service is their strong suit— they tend to be great rainmakers. As our client base gets more diverse, we find that we require more diversity of skills and points-of-view in the firm."

Looking for Passion

Olsson's staff— not its executive leadership— drives strategic decisions like entering new markets. "We look for passion from the people in the business units," explains Severin. "We'd rather enter a marginal market with super-motivated people who want to make it work than a great market with indifferent people." Sometimes it doesn't work and the firm makes mistakes but it is not afraid to make them and it refuses to hold people back.

"The grass-roots nature of how we develop new markets works because our people decide where their passions lie," says McManus. "As an executive, my role is to detect overlaps where groups may be stumbling over each other to seize new opportunities. It's a clear positive when you have people moving and thinking the same way in new business development because it really increases the chances of success."

Opportunities for Leadership

When you have dozens of small business units in a large firm, you create many more opportunities for leadership and responsibility than in a top-down firm. Olsson employees take on leadership and responsibility much sooner than they would have expected in a firm of its size. "It's amazing how many young people are leaders in this firm right now," comments Severin.

So many Millennial leaders require mentoring and coaching to get them to reach their full potential. Olsson has initiatives underway to identify people that the executive firm leadership would like to engage in intensive career development. "It seems that underperformers get all of management's attention," says McManus. "We need to start paying significant attention to the highest achievers and help them be the best they can be, too."

Being placed in environments where they can be responsible and accountable, exert leadership skills, and follow their passion makes working at Olsson very compelling for young engineers-- but there are many other things that the firm does that make it a good fit. Ownership opportunities and performance-based compensation are available to everyone. "We're a highly positive, high energy organization," says McManus "We want everyone to know that their contribution in valued." One concrete way Olsson does this is by vesting staff 100% in the firm's 401(k) plan from the first day of employment. "We don't want people to stay if the firm is not a good fit for them just because they want to become vested in the plan."

The Last Interaction

Severin says that clients' experiences are only as good as their last interaction with the firm. "We view client relationships as collaborative. Clients today want to be more involved and they are looking for options-oriented partners, not people who think they are doing projects in a vacuum. We expect our people to be in constant communications with the clients."

Olsson facilitates this by allowing business units to pick and choose their own clients. "There are rare occasions that we are just not on the same page with a client," says Severin. "If enough business units choose not to work with a specific client, the group makes a decision in whether we keep him or her as a client."

Olsson also has a systematic feedback loop with clients that is managed by someone from the firm that is not part of the project. "The person who does this is a former newspaper reporter," explains Severin. "She's good at getting the real story. She notices things like client body language and doesn't let it rest if he thinks there might be a problem. We could use more people with that skill set."

The Value is in the "What Else"?

Another advantage of the small business units is they are able to identify areas where they can be more efficient and drive down costs as a response to downward pressure on prices. Firm management is committed to providing the infrastructure to facilitate this. It also helps that the business units are very effective at client selection and avoiding commodity-driven markets.

"Most clients think an engineer is an engineer is an engineer; the technical skill of the engineer has been commoditized," explains Severin. "So what else is there you are offering? If the answer is nothing, then you are providing low value.

"If the client sees himself as part of a collaborative process and a team of impassioned players, then that's where the value is-- and the clients are willing to pay for it."

PHILLIPS ARCHITECTURE:
TRAINING THE NEXT GENERATION

Phillips Architecture is a 30-person architecture and interior design firm based in Raleigh, North Carolina. Here are some keys to the firm's consistent 17-year success:

Focus on Value

Phillips' aim is to provide the highest level of expertise in their region for the design of commercial office space. While a full service architectural firm, the firm's market niche has allowed it to focus on providing a comprehensive set of specialized services for its clients. An example of this focus is the customized design software the firm has built to enhance their work's quality and consistency. With over 50 regular clients, each with a different set of preferences for workflow, Phillips' managers and designers benefit from the software which helps guide each project to match the preferences of each individual client. Clients like the personalized attention, designers like making fewer mistakes, and the firm's principals appreciate the increased value of client loyalty.

Planning Work

Phillips engages large numbers of small-to-medium projects for a core group of diversely oriented clients. Monday morning scheduling meetings allocate team members for special needs, but most assignments are made spontaneously by the team leaders during the week as soon as client needs are known. The team leaders have full authority to set their teams, including outside engineers, to most effectively handle their projects. The firm's processes are standardized for consistency, but were also designed to be general in nature to give the team leaders and members latitude in choosing the path that best fits the situation. Many of the firm's projects are small— with fees around $30K— and often appear with little advance notice, but an urgent need for quick completion. The firm is able to plan work and allocate resources with some precision for about a three-week window and beyond that, it makes educated judgments based on trends they have identified over time. With so many short-term projects, how does Phillips handle project management?

Train 'em Up

Phillips has five project team leaders that train Millennial members and empower them to be real players with projects very early on in the design process. New designers learn how to manage project tasks quickly and, by dealing directly with clients, have a sense of personal responsibility for the project's success. Each designer is assisted by firm principals to guide, teach, and encourage the flexibility that allows the designer to adjust their efforts to the particular needs of the each client. How does this strategy play with new team members?

Success is a Two-Way Street

Junior people appear to benefit from being allowed into the project's critical path early, because they are being encouraged to build an understanding of their clients' goals and preferences. The importance of learning the mechanics of a project's process, as well as the more popular design and management skills, teaches team members valuable lessons in efficiency and effectiveness. This balance of emphasis tends to create quicker response times to client requests, less wasted time in producing a project, and a relaxed sense of urgency that often dilutes a designer's focus on the more subjective and aesthetic components of their project. This focus on caring for clients tends to produce a prosperous business environment that is shared through annual bonuses.

Staff Time is a Precious Commodity

Phillips provides a catered lunch to its staff at least two days a week and has a break room full of firm-provided food and drinks every day. Catered lunches serve as team meeting and training sessions. The lunches are convenient and popular with the team members and they have developed a sense of ownership about using the time together productively. A benefit to the firm is that on in-house lunch days staff are available to take client calls and unexpected client visits. Also, there is a sense that eating together helps people to feel, think, and behave like a group-- and contributes positively to the overall firm culture.

A Loose/Tight Culture

While Phillips takes its helpfulness to its clients seriously and expends significant time and cost to collect or create the most effective tools for their team, the goal of creating a relaxed environment around the office helps the designers deal more effectively with the challenges and stresses that the job can bring. Phillips offers flexible work schedules, work from home as needed, birthday parties, a very effective Fun Committee, relaxed dress code, full-time assistants, and the autonomy for each person to create their personal space and style.

An Associate Answers the Phone

The receptionist at Phillips is an associate with the firm. Clients know and trust her. While everyone in the organization has a direct line, most clients call the main number because they know that the person who answers the phone will help them in a way that no voice mail system can ever match. This human touch is supplemented by a Phillips-built automated software program that displays everyone's schedule and current status so that staff and clients know how to find anyone when needed. Clients have total access to the firm's members when they have questions or concerns. Phillips would rather know about a client problem sooner rather than later so they can orchestrate a productive response as quickly as possible.

Managing Growth Effectively

Phillips takes a two-pronged approach to hiring. It hires slowly and has candidates meet with several groups of team members to collect a variety of feedback. It also employs non-intrusive behavioral preferences tests to help identify the best matches. Candidates get a copy of their report and the reports of various firm members so they can best understand and respond to the information. Often these responses provide valuable insights to assist in making the optimum hiring decisions for both parties. These same reports are used by the various teams to foster greater understanding of optimum work styles of team members.

Does this approach work? You bet. Phillips had zero turnover in 2005 and, in over 15 years in business, has never had a layoff.

QUAD KNOPF, INC.: HIRING FOR GROWTH

Quad Knopf, Inc. is a 360-person engineering and planning services firm based in Visalia, California.

In 1998, Quad Knopf merged into a single firm and since then, the firm has achieved 25% to 30% revenue growth annually by leveraging a combination of the right services, clients, people, and geographic work areas. Their principal challenge has been to change in ways that maximize growth and make the most out of new business opportunities—without overtaxing the firm's infrastructure and cash flow.

A Strategic Approach to Hiring for Growth

For professional services firms, hiring new staff takes a big bite out of cash flow and can really threaten the financial health of the company. Historically, Quad Knopf had relaxed expectations regarding the assimilation of new staff into the firm. They typically allowed 4-6 weeks for people to connect and get fully involved in working on project teams.

For Quad Knopf, the costs (e.g., recruitment, equipment, etc.) of hiring 120 new employees in a single year resulted in the financial equivalent of taking the revenue produced by a 60-person firm out of its cash flow. The firm needed to mitigate the adverse financial effects caused by this intense growth.

The firm decided to implement a constrained hiring plan to ensure that it didn't add more people than it was able to assimilate and thus cause undue financial stress. At first, the firm simply adopted a specific hiring plan for each branch office, but this did not entirely address the problem. In response to continuing challenges to the company's cash flow, weekly meetings were initiated between the recruiting staff and the company president. Placing more central control over the process has dramatically improved the quality of the candidates being recruited. President Mike Knopf believes that the process caused hiring managers to do a better job of assessing the need for new hires as well as providing better screening of candidates for the right fit for the firm and the job being filled. But this change did not address the entire problem. In order to reduce the turnover rate and improve employee satisfaction, the firm needed to improve the way they assimilated new people.

Getting People Engaged Quicker

In order to maintain solid growth while preserving the firm's culture, quality service, and profitability, Quad Knopf had to take on the challenge of getting people up-to-speed faster. One problem in the old way of assimilating new employees was that "everyone thought that someone else was doing it." Today, the firm has institutionalized mentoring and coaching in a team environment.

The firm conducts a series of new hire orientations. One is with the business services director to get people up to speed on important housekeeping details. Another is with the company's senior management team who offers firm history and a comprehensive overview of the firm's client types, the services it offers, profiles of the branch offices, and the firm's philosophy. They also get an overview of financial metrics so they have an immediate connection to overall firm goals. Quad Knopf is a transparent organization. Other than salary data, the firm provides ongoing access to budget, profit goals, revenue, and other financial information. All of these things help Quad Knopf achieve its objective of getting people into the critical path as soon as possible.

Recent employee surveys and other feedback show that the firm culture is more uniform today than a year ago. Employees old and new identify with Quad Knopf culture more strongly and turnover has gone down dramatically. The process of hiring more selectively coupled with the process of getting people engaged more quickly and reducing turnover has lessened the stress that growth has historically placed on cash flow.

Learning to Communicate

Quad Knopf figured that it could do even better to ensure long-term employee satisfaction and productivity. Twenty volunteers recently studied the issue of communication between the firm and its employees and made recommendations to management. It turned out that people wanted information that would allow individuals to assess specifically how their work was contributing to the overall productivity and profitability of the firm. "People were getting the puzzle pieces," Knopf explains, "but what they really wanted was access to the picture on the puzzle box."

The firm initiated a process in which anyone who was interested could participate equally in a forum that explored and confirmed the roles and the impacts individual people had in the organization. The exercise and others like it, provided lots of opportunities for people to exert and exercise leadership. Knopf has watched leaders emerge out of this environment. "This process is significant to me because it helps the management team redirect leaders to higher levels of effectiveness in the firm," says Knopf.

It's Not about One Person

The clear pattern that has contributed most significantly to Quad Knopf's success is that management understands that it is essential for staff to be involved in making significant improvements. "I don't want the firm's success to reside in one person— I want to tap into the intelligence and diversity of the staff and leverage their ideas, their energy, and their passion," explains Knopf.

In fact, when Quad Knopf analyzes its competitors, it finds it easy to identify the firms where all the strength and power reside in just one person. "These firms are doing great work and we don't take that away from them," Knopf says, "but they are not the firms that we'll be competing with as we evaluate and pursue new markets and opportunities. They are, for the most part, at the limits of their capacity. Firms that feature empowered employees expand beyond the strength of their leaders— these firms will be our competition as we grow our business."

Enlightened Business Development

"Quad Knopf does not focus on getting new work," Knopf says. "We focus on establishing more client relationships." To illustrate his point, Mike offers the following (typical) scenario:

"Let's say a project manager is struggling to deal with the details of a proposal for a potential project. The contract will include an unacceptable clause that the prospective client won't back away from or perhaps the client is demonstrating some other indication that he sees the firm's service as a commodity and fails to see how Quad Knopf can provide true value to the project. I will ask the project manager: 'Are you busy? Do you *need* more work right now? Or are you looking for a valued client relationship? This client is not looking for a relationship. Why are you doing this?'

"The point is that Quad Knopf is looking to bring value to the project— for the profession, for the public, and for the client. There is a huge demand for the firm's services— but clients have to be willing to allow us to provide value to them. At the same time, we recognize that we won't have an opportunity to do that unless we can also show that we understand the client's issues and are willing to align our approach with the client's needs and concerns."

In order for any firm to do this, there needs to be a process of building trust and understanding among clients and the service provider. Quad Knopf uses its work as a platform for demonstrating the value it adds to the project. Quality work that solves clients' problems is what sells value. Recently, the firm asked representatives of all its client groups to come and talk with their staff about two things: what challenges do they face that the firm could help them with, and what does the staff need to hear from the clients to help them be more effective in fulfilling their client's needs? When the clients left, the staff assembled in breakout groups to discuss consistent messages that they heard, surprises, and things they didn't know about clients. At the end of the event, there was a survey gauging its effectiveness. Knopf explains, "One hundred percent of the participants found the exercise valuable and we have been able to use this event as a platform to reinforce other efforts to improve the company."

Doable, but Not Easy

"Affecting change in a large firm is like turning an aircraft carrier— it requires a significant amount of time as well as planning. But once processes are in place and they are demonstrated to improve outcomes, it's possible to effect change in large organizations," concludes Knopf.

VANDERWEIL ENGINEERS, INC.:
ALWAYS TRYING TO GET BETTER

Vanderweil Engineers, Inc. is a 320-person multi-disciplinary consulting engineering firm specializing in mechanical, electrical and plumbing engineering for buildings, central heating and chiller plants, power generation, and transmission and distribution design based in Boston, Massachusetts. Keith Lord, the firm's chief financial officer, shares their story.

Proceeding with Caution

Prior to the economic downturn immediately following 9/11, Vanderweil was structured in a much different way in terms of overhead and its infrastructure. After the downturn, the firm was compelled to make some hard decisions which included reducing its overhead drastically and "right-sizing" the firm. There were a few lean years during this restructuring process, but the firm's commitment to client service never wavered and its focus on overhead and running the business helped set the firm back on the right track. "We were able to restructure our firm by having the right people in the right positions which allowed us to operate much more efficiently with fewer people" explains Lord.

One thing that the firm has changed is how it approaches business development. Whereas in the past, the firm had staff that focused on purely selling, its model today is based much more on a "seller-doer" approach. "Ninety percent of our work comes from repeat clients," Lord says. "The principals who generate new projects from our clients are also billable to projects and they stay very much involved. Business development is tied into client relationship and our backlog has never been stronger". What about the other 10% of the business? Vanderweil has developed a brand name for certain types of work and between that and the referrals from former clients, they generate the remainder of the business for them. It also has long-term relationships with owners directly and often get the opportunity to refer their architectural partners for projects.

Growing the firm is a strong priority but based on its history and tradition they are proceeding with caution. "We are constantly watching the business indicators and as much as possible try to match our staff to the workload. We also have an opportunity to be a bit more selective on the work that we do and focus on the type of work at which we have the strongest competency. To us, it is more about the client relationship and the type of work rather than the project size" says Eli Sherman, the firm's president.

"It would be easy for us to take on work at a greater pace and bring on additional staff to do it. But once again, we want to make sure that we grow for the right reasons and not jeopardize our reputation by delivering less quality work to our clients," continues Sherman.

Leveraging Experience

Vanderweil is fortunate to have a large number of experienced people who have been with the firm for a long time and who Lord calls "the foundation of our business."

"We recently held our 10-year luncheon for the firm," Lord explains, "and it was eye-opening to realize that there were 88 people out of just over 300 who have been with the firm for more than 10 years— many with much more than that and some even approaching 40 years!"

What makes them stay? "Let's face it, our staff gets calls every day trying to lure them away," says Lord. "It is true that we offer our people a very competitive compensation package, but that's only part of the story. We provide them an opportunity to succeed and how far they go in our firm is entirely up to them."

Another piece of the story is the work that Vanderweil is doing. "Our people want to work on interesting projects and, right now, we are everywhere-- we have projects from Boston to Las Vegas to Singapore. The nature of the work we pursue and we win is compelling to our staff," explains Sherman.

What makes people want to come to Vanderweil? The firm is committed to keeping overhead low— not an easy task with offices in high-rent areas like downtown Boston and Alexandria, Virginia— but it is always looking at everything from insurance premiums to UPS and office supply charges to negotiate better deals. They plow much of what they save into employee benefits and salaries.

Vanderweil is also committed to mentoring and training its employees. This helps the firm bring in Millennial engineers and helps them accelerate their careers. "We know that we are going to lose some people along the way and we can't keep everyone. Although we do not like the idea of being the training ground for some people, we get so much out of the people that stay with us that the investment of training and mentoring is money well-spent."

Always Trying to get Better

Vanderweil understands that it must constantly evolve to continue to succeed and grow. "We need to stay in tune with the industry trends in terms of the way buildings are being designed today. Buildings are getting to be much more complex and there is a great deal more emphasis today on energy efficiency. We need to make certain that we provide responsible engineering to our clients," says Sherman.

The firm is also looking into employee ownership to further entice staff with Vanderweil long-term. "Our key people are the business drivers— people who bring in the work and outstanding technical people are our greatest asset and we'll do what we can to keep them," explains Lord.

FINAL THOUGHTS

"Even the most grandiose strategies must eventually degenerate into work."

– Peter Drucker

I mentioned previously my wife's observations concerning the philosophy of magazines offering parental advice which for years has encouraged parents to put their children in every activity under the sun in order to make them well-rounded. Within the past few years, however, she has noticed an abrupt shift. Now, the 'experts' in these magazines tell you to take the opposite approach. Kids, these experts now say should not be overstimulated but must have significant unstructured time in which to play and explore.

Ah, the cycle continues as the pendulum swings back. Certainly, the next generation to follow the Millennials, now being called Generation Z, will be as strange and foreign to Millennials as they are to us. At least there is some satisfaction in the form of payback. Before you know it, the 'kids' in your office now will be moaning about 'the kids coming out of school today.'

In any time period, there are always challenges to running a successful business. The challenges may change, and often do, but firms that excel in any era are always the ones who are 'ahead of their time.' Very early in my career, one of my Veterans generation bosses once shared a story that still resonates to this day. When he was much younger, he and another engineer were working for the same firm and quickly becoming rising stars in their organization. After time, however, they both grew frustrated with the slow pace of change and financial rewards they believed were not commensurate with the level of profits they were bringing in. Eventually, they came to the conclusion they could do it better.

So, they set off on their own and formed a partnership. In the end, they found out they were correct in their assumptions. They were able to do it better than their previous firm, which is now out of business, and they had succeeded for many years. Now, with much wisdom obtained from many years in the business, my boss said he realized that young people in his firm would look at what they were doing and also believe they could do it better. And, in reality, he continued, they were probably right. To him, he believed he had figured out the circle of life in the A/E business.

When he first shared this story, I found it intriguing, yet its moral escaped me. However, after ruminating over his message for almost 20 years, I believe he was on to something, although the message has universal organizational application beyond the A/E business, or even business in general.

Capitalism, as an economic system, has many faults. For one, I learned through my economics professor when studying for my Master's Degree that the real driver of capitalism is 'greed.' Economist rely on what they believe is people's innate desire to acquire. Consumers purchase because they want more stuff, so they work hard to be able to consume hard. Greed is certainly not the most noble of goals.

Winston Churchill said, "Capitalism is a terrible economic system…the only ones worse are all of the others." He's right. I had the unique opportunity of visiting consulting engineering firms in Russia after the fall of communism and also firms in Belarus, the last country in Europe still using the Marxist model. It was depressing to see engineers of all ages sitting in antiquated offices with outdated equipment having little work to do. I'll never forget the looks of despair on their faces.

All they ever remembered was communism. The government told them what to do, when to do it, how to do it, how much they would get paid for doing it, and what they would buy with that money. Now, in an instant, everything changed. Never in North America have we experienced change on this scale. In the former Soviet Bloc, generations of professionals do not know how to think for themselves. I made some friends on this trip and kept in touch over the years. Sadly, they are still struggling with figuring out how to operate in this new world. I don't know about you, but I'll take capitalism any day.

I've noticed in A/E firms, other businesses, and even non-profit organizations such as churches, they all are started by people with a vision for the future who recognize many existing organizations are not adapting to the changes in society or the economic landscape. These entrepreneurs believe 'they can do it better.' In a lot of cases, they are correct. However, sometimes it takes many tries. This is the result of our capitalistic system.

A friend of mine, Mike Taylor of Taylor Engineering in Spokane, Washington, is one of these individuals. He started an engineering firm in the 1970s because he 'believed he could do it better.' Problem was he also believed by virtue of being an engineer he also knew how to run a business. He was wrong and had to shut the doors.

However, that did not stop him. A couple of years later, and many years wiser, he tried again. This time, he found traction and went on to build a firm that has grown over the past 25 years to 60 people and has a great reputation among its client base and in the communities in which it operates. Mike did it differently. Not only did he begin his firm with fresh ideas, but he always tried to stay on top of change before change overcame him. Even to this day, he is constantly looking for new 'best practices' to implement.

Mike has been very successful, but he did not get there alone. Mike took others with him, and that's the key. This message of this book is Winning *With* Millennials. Mike created an organization and culture where bright, talented, and motivated engineers could find a home and thrive. In 2008, Mike completed a 10-year transition plan in which he now no longer owns any part of the company and is not an employee of the firm.

As I talked with Mike about this change, I saw emotions bubbling up within him. This was his baby. His blood, sweat, tears, first marriage, first heart attack, and the equity in his home all went to building Taylor Engineering. In fact, it is his namesake. However, I also saw in Mike a sense of pride in what has been accomplished, a sense of fulfillment in the significant number of people he has brought along with him, and a sense of confidence in the leadership team that was taking the helm.

Bill Gates was once asked by a reporter if he felt guilty for becoming a billionaire. Without hesitation, he replied, "No, I just think of all the many millionaires that were created because of Microsoft." Both Mike and Bill won with people. Dr. John Maxwell, after studying leadership for 30 years, said "I'm convinced that you can find no example in history of anyone who did anything significant totally alone." Don't try to be the first to break the trend. It can't be done.

Mike, and his firm, is a product of capitalism. The system is designed to take entrepreneurs with the best ideas and direct 'capital' in their direction. Like food to a teenager, the results are they grow, sometimes rapidly. Capitalism, however, is relentless on those organizations who refuse to grow and change with the times. Eventually 'capital,' both financial and human, are redirected to more productive enterprises and these firms cease to exist.

The success of Mike's 'former' firm in the future is now dependent on the new leadership's ability to continue to change with the times and push the envelope. If they ever drop the ball, eventually Millennials and the generations behind them will also think they can do it better. Mike himself will tell you that starting a design firm is hard work. Building a lasting and perpetual legacy through a design firm, one that continues well beyond its founder, is even harder and rarer. HKS, mentioned previously, is one such example.

I believe Mike has done an excellent job of instilling solid principles and building a strong leadership transition team that will successfully continue his legacy, but only time will tell. In addition, the real test is how well the current firm's leaders do in making the next transition.

This is what excites me about the subject of this book. To build a legacy, you have to win with people. I want to win with people! I want to bring them along with me! I also want to encourage you to take advantage of the tremendous generation coming out of today's colleges and universities. Morph your firm into one that will both attract them and provide an environment where they can thrive throughout their careers. Also, prepare them for the changes that must be continually made to achieve these goals when future generations arrive at our doorsteps.

Now get out there, create your own legacy and win with Millennials!

Printed in the United States
128814LV00001B/2/P